# After This

Alice Nelson is an Australian writer. Her first novel, *The Last Sky*, was shortlisted for *The Australian*/Vogel's Literary Award, won the T.A.G. Hungerford Award and was shortlisted for the Australian Society of Authors' Barbara Jefferis Award. She was named Best Young Australian Novelist of 2009 in the *Sydney Morning Herald*'s national awards program. Alice works as a freelance journalist and teaches creative writing. She is currently completing her doctorate in the School of English and Cultural Studies at the University of Western Australia.

# After This

*Survivors of the Holocaust speak*

# ALICE NELSON

First published 2015 by
FREMANTLE PRESS
25 Quarry Street, Fremantle 6160
(PO Box 158, North Fremantle 6159)
Western Australia
www.fremantlepress.com.au

Copyright © Alice Nelson, 2015

The moral rights of the author have been asserted.

This book is copyright. Apart from any fair dealing for the purpose of private study, research, criticism or review, as permitted under the Copyright Act, no part may be reproduced by any process without written permission. Enquiries should be made to the publisher.

Consultant editor: Naama Amram
Cover design: Nada Backovic
Typesetting: Karmen Lee

Front cover photographs (clockwise from top left): Rosa Levy with parents; Heiny Ellert (right) at Feldafing displaced persons camp; Kurt Ehrenfeld with father and sister in 1943.

Cover images: background texture © Boonsom/Shutterstock; background texture © David M. Schrader/Shutterstock; blossom © Feblacal/Dreamstime.com; barbed wire © Tshanahans/Dreamstime.com.

A catalogue record for this book is available from the National Library of Australia

ISBN 9781925162356 (paperback)
ISBN 9781925162370 (ebook)

Fremantle Press is supported by the Western Australian State Government through the Department of Cultural Industries, Tourism and Sport..

Publication of this title was assisted by the Commonwealth Government through Creative Australia, its arts funding and advisory body.

# Contents

Foreword by Arnold Zable ................................................. 7
Introductory essay by Alice Nelson ............................... 10

Betty Niesten ........................................................................ 19
Isaac (Henk) Piller ............................................................... 38
Fryda Grynberg ..................................................................... 58
Bill Glatzer ............................................................................. 73
Rosalie Rothschild ............................................................... 88
Rosa Levy ............................................................................. 114
Aaron Landau ..................................................................... 138
Erica Moen .......................................................................... 146
Kurt Ehrenfeld ................................................................... 170
Anonymous ......................................................................... 192
Chaim Majteles .................................................................. 206
Richard Farago .................................................................. 220
Hanoch (Heiny) Ellert ...................................................... 249
Pola Potaznik ..................................................................... 270

Glossary .............................................................................. 282
Acknowledgements ......................................................... 286

# Foreword

These life-stories are extraordinary. The telling is straightforward. There is no artifice, no embroidery. Each narrative is a recounting of specific events set in specific places, told matter-of-factly. The facts speak for themselves. The cumulative effect is riveting. It is a mitzvah these eyewitness accounts have been assembled and put between the covers. Made solid. The darkness made visible.

I am of the second generation. As a child I heard anecdotes, fragments of family stories, gazed at photos of grandparents, uncles and aunts, cousins, scenes of my parents' home-city of Bialystok and its surrounding towns and villages. The prewar photos were haunting, as are the prewar photos that accompany the stories in this anthology. The images are rescued from oblivion.

They add immeasurably to the telling. It was a wise decision to publish them.

My parents, and many of their generation, split their lives between two periods: before the war and after the war. So it is with these accounts. Each tale unfolds as a three-act drama. Act one is set in the time before: Once upon a time I had a home, a family. A mother, a father, brothers and sisters, a circle of friends, extended family. Once I had a life, a community, and a sense of belonging.

Then all is overturned. Ruptured. For some, the second act is a drawn-out process of accumulating horrors. It may include years of slave labour, incarceration in a succession of ghettoes, concentration camps, countless acts of cruelty. For others the second act begins abruptly with a knock on the door, a herding into the streets, a trek to the railway station, deportation to death camps. For all, it is a descent into hell.

Act two ends at the moment of liberation. But the impact endures. Prewar life has been shattered. Freedom is coupled with a sense of devastation. Emptiness. Accompanied by confirmation of the death of loved ones. Survivors return to homes occupied by others, to decimated communities. Hence, act three begins in uncertainty, a state of limbo, with time spent in displaced persons camps, journeys to new worlds, to the ends of the earth, to Perth, distant Melbourne. It encompasses years of rebuilding, creating new lives, raising families.

New photos appear, family portraits snapped at gatherings and weddings. Images of rebirth, new links in severed family chains forged through hard work and a ferocious determination. The memories and trauma, however, cannot be suppressed. The survivors' stories invariably emerge after years of silence, maintained to protect their children from the horrors, or because their experiences seem so out of place in the bright light of the new world. In many cases, it is only the urgent request of children grown to adulthood that prises open the Pandora's box.

In time, the reluctant narrators begin to see a deeper purpose. They embody history. They are eyewitnesses. And they bear witness. Some begin to address schools, the public, and become guides into the Kingdom of Darkness. The Holocaust Institute of Western Australia, its scribes and volunteer interviewers, and Alice Nelson, act as midwives, facilitating the rebirth of suppressed memory.

These accounts, when read in total, represent collective wisdom. They have much to say about love, hatred, trauma, betrayal, endurance, the randomness of fate, the pain of separation, the extremes of human brutality and perversion. And, in some instances, they touch upon unexpected kindnesses, enacted by those who risked their lives to save a fellow human being. As one writer says, in response to a life-saving act by a stranger: 'It was the first time I had experienced that there were good people in the world.'

These accounts, however, do not offer an easy way out. The trauma, the tragedy and the brutality are not diminished, not sanitised. The horrors are named and documented. They are not made more palatable. We are compelled to listen.

I leave the final word to one of the narrators. It is typically direct and prosaic: 'The Holocaust is a monumental part of history, so please do not forget what I am saying. I won't be here forever to tell the story. It is in your hands and the hands of your generation and generations to come – to always remember.'

Arnold Zable

## *Introductory essay*

On the front page of my husband's family photograph album is the black-and-white image of an old Polish rabbi. This man, with his dark eyes, his full beard and his extraordinary prescience, saved my husband's grandfather from a terrible fate by convincing him to leave Poland and arranging passage out of the country before it was too late to leave. All of those who came after in my husband's family owe their lives to this scholarly rabbi – all the Australian and Israeli and American descendants, my own husband, the two strapping boys who clomp down the hallways of our home on the quiet shores of Australia, and the children that they themselves might one day have.

Jewish history is threaded with peril and deliverance, persecution and survival, miracles and catastrophes.

The Holocaust – colossal in scale and recent in memory – is so charged with horror and so obsessively represented that it has become almost legendary. It is a history that sometimes feels too overwhelming to be contemplated. In our family the photograph of the long-dead rabbi has become a way to make the distant miracle of escape something more concrete and tangible. It is a small antidote to the abstractions of history. Another future – which most likely would have been no future – was frighteningly possible. The photograph of the rabbi, sitting as it does alongside images of family weddings, laughing children, beach picnics and bar mitzvahs, is a solemn reminder of this.

We seek them out, these tangible mementoes that help us to touch up against the memory of the Holocaust, to relate to it as something more than an historical allegory of inhumanity. Perhaps it's the same impulse that draws so many people to the sites of the death camps and to Holocaust museums all over the world to see for ourselves the piles of abandoned shoes, the shorn hair, the cases full of spectacles, the relics and remnants of destruction. It's also what makes us listen to the stories of those who survived the conflagration. For the most part, I believe that this is more than a voyeuristic impulse or a desire for tangible proof of the compressed cargo of terror that is the legacy of the Holocaust. We listen to and read the testimonies of the survivors because we know that it is important to understand – as far as understanding is possible – the lived human reality of the Holocaust, and to bear witness in some way for those who emerged from its crucible.

We are fast approaching the juncture at which living memory of the Holocaust must be relinquished. Those survivors still among us are reaching the end of their natural life spans and soon our human conduit to the events of seventy years ago will be erased. How do we think about the Shoah from this lengthening distance? How do we contemplate its terrible lessons in a time when there will no longer be survivors among us? For too many, the Holocaust has already attained the status of a mythical phenomenon; something at once too known and completely unknowable, too incomprehensible in its dimensions, in its sheer numbers. Of course there are the atrocious photographs, the appalling statistics, the Holocaust museums and memorials, the huge amassing of documentary testimony, the endless texts and films and representations. But it is too easy for the stretch of years between now and then to insulate us from those anonymous victims, for a numinous remoteness to settle irrevocably over the events.

There is a hefty body of theory about the ethics and aesthetics of remembrance, a ceaseless fraught philosophical debate about the impossibility of true communication of the singular horror of the Shoah. In a passionate condemnation of the manipulations and perversions of memory, Holocaust survivor and unparalleled chronicler Elie Wiesel cautions about the transformation of memory into a more palatable reality. The accounts of the survivors, he has argued – the diaries and narratives and recordings – are the best way to ensure faithfulness to memory. 'Listen to the survivors and respect their wounded sensibility,' he implores us. 'Open yourselves to their scarred memory, and mingle your tears with theirs.'

The fourteen narratives included in this collection have been wrested from those scarred memories. Beneath the words on the pages here, so painfully translated, is the quivering presence of that undiminished trauma. In many ways the narratives are disastrously alike. Recollections of round-ups and cattle wagons, beatings and starvation, camps and ovens, run through the testimonies like dark leitmotifs. These people were subject to unspeakable brutality. They were starved, humiliated, tortured, tattooed and stripped of everything that defined them. They watched their friends and family members being whipped, clubbed, shot, herded into gas chambers. Concussed by what they had endured and by the uneasy miracle of their own survival, they returned to home towns empty of their Jewish communities, to a world that they could never again look upon with the same eyes.

These personal depositions help to refract the overwhelming statistics and abstractions of history into the specific details of one little Dutch boy stripped of his family, his home and his name and forced into hiding, one terrified Polish girl hidden in the stifling crawlspace of a hayloft, one Lithuanian man who was branded with not one but two tattooed numbers because the initial one was not deemed clear enough. The fourteen survivors whose stories are included here are not abstractions, they are not anonymous faces to be flicked past in the all too familiar black-and-white photographs of the history books. They are daughters and sons and brothers and mothers and aunts and cousins – people who live out their lives in the peaceful suburbs of Australia.

For many of the survivors whose stories are included in this collection, the telling only came late in life. In the years after the war their energies were focused on the present – the further displacements of emigration, the challenges of transposing their lives into a new language and a new culture, the raising of children, the creation of homes and businesses. Their new lives demanded that they remain silent, that they not trouble the still waters of their adopted Australian communities with their unwelcome tales of the abyss. Even those who tried to tell their stories faltered in the face of the sheer incomprehensibility of their experience, the inchoate nature of the knowledge they bore. What they had endured was too awful to be assimilated into narratives, too unbelievable to be understood by anyone who had not also been there. How could any words penetrate the circle of flames from which they had stepped, miraculously alive? How could they ever adequately describe the forbidding terrain in which they had dwelt for so long?

A silence may have surrounded the war years, but it was a fraught and densely populated silence. Though the survivors could not always speak coherently about what they had endured, the haunting revenants of that experience escaped in whispers, in fragments, in the screams of nightmares and in the emanations of fear that filtered through to their children. Deep, quivering threads of anxiety stretched beneath the everydayness of their lives. After what they had been through, they could not fully believe in the existence of a benign world and they clung to their children fiercely. How could they ever communicate to them the most profound parts of their history? In the Jewish tradition, to remember is a holy act, a conduit between generations, but all the old rituals and familiar observances had been torn away from the survivors. The weight of the dead pressed too heavily on them to be shared with their Australian children.

The writer Leah Kaminsky, daughter of a survivor of Bergen-Belsen, has written powerfully about the burden carried by the children of survivors, the deeply embedded fears and chaos of emotion that formed an often unspoken legacy, and the struggle of the next generation to excavate their own stories, their own identities, from underneath the layers of trauma within their families. In a poem entitled 'My daughter goes on camp', Kaminsky writes about the haunting resonances that certain words take on even decades later, in quiet countries far from Europe.

*when will I know quiet joy?*
*when will school camp be school camp*
*a train just a train, an oven just an oven?*
*when will I let them go*
*knowing they will come back?*

The Israeli writer David Grossman, who grew up among Holocaust survivors in Jerusalem in the years after the war, tells the story of a family member – a survivor of Treblinka – who arrived at his wedding with a bandage on her forearm covering her tattooed number. She did not want to cast a shadow over the celebration with this bleak souvenir of the camps, this dark amulet of the Shoah. Throughout the ceremony, Grossman found himself unable to take his eyes away from the bandage. 'I understood then, very sharply,' he wrote, 'how much all of us here in Israel are walking on a surface as thin as that bandage, under which lies a void that threatens, every moment, to drag down our daily lives, our illusion of routine.'

The survivors had made a profound and extraordinary effort, in the face of everything they knew about humanity, to continue to choose life, to live on and raise families and start businesses and grow vegetables and bake cakes and attend shule. They forged new and outwardly successful lives and tried as best they could not to dwell on the chasm from which they had emerged.

It has been said that history is a race between education and catastrophe. In 1990, when most of the survivors were already in their sixties and seventies, the Holocaust Institute of Western Australia was founded by Dr Ben Korman OAM and a small group of volunteers. They were compelled to preserve the memory of the Holocaust in an effort to ensure that its dark legacy was not lost and that we would continue to ponder the particular knowledge that the Holocaust has bequeathed us. The Institute was not designed to be a static museum, but a place of encounter where Holocaust survivors would recount their experience to visitors and answer their questions, where Western Australians could gain a profound living sense of the human realities of that particular history.

Volunteers from the fledgling Holocaust Institute met with those survivors who were willing to participate in the endeavour and interviewed them about their wartime experiences. For many, it was the first time they had transposed their stories into any sort of coherent narrative, the first time they had shared their stories beyond the circle of their families. Some had not told their own children the terrible details they shared with the scribes from the Holocaust Institute.

When the Holocaust Institute opened its public

program, which was particularly targeted at school students, the survivors formed a roster, signing on week after week, month after month, to read their testimony and answer questions. They had not been able to bury their dead, to say Kaddish or sit shiva for them, and, for many of the survivors, recounting their stories became a kind of commemoration that had not been available to them before. No redemption could ever be possible and to speak of healing or catharsis belies the horrifying enormity of their experiences, but all the survivors who volunteered at the Holocaust Institute felt that their work was important and necessary. They all firmly held the belief that sharing their experiences, no matter how painful for them, was a way to counteract apathy as well as forgetfulness. After all the years of silence, the survivors took comfort in the thought that their memories were being placed in the hands of another generation.

The narratives included here are extended versions of the testimonies shared by the survivors at the Holocaust Institute. They have been presented as narrated by the survivors themselves; they are not intended to be pieces of literature, but unadorned recountings of experience.

Levie Lever, the father of Dutch survivor Betty Niesten whose story is included in this collection, scrawled a few words on a postcard and tossed it from the window of the cattle train that was transporting his family across the country towards Auschwitz. *Dear Family,* he wrote. *We are on transport. Tell it to others. We hope to come back.*

The stories in this collection are, in their own way, a series of letters scrawled from the haunting traces of memory. Letters tossed from the window of a sealed train to an unknowing and neglectful world where people kept on sowing their fields and mending their fences as the cattle cars lumbered by full of their desperate human cargo. These are letters written with terror, with desperation and, ultimately, with the hope that they might be read and understood.

*Tell it to others*, a doomed man wrote. With their precise details of human lives bent out of shape by a horrifying history, these narratives are at once a bulwark against forgetting, a warning and an inheritance. *I am here. I endured*, they whisper to us.

As the Holocaust recedes in time, as the last living witnesses to its terrible memory pass from the world, it becomes ever more important to listen to the stories of survivors. To listen and attend and remember.

## Betty Niesten

I was born in Amsterdam in the Netherlands on the third of April 1913. My sister Judith Lever was born on 22 January 1912 and was only fourteen months older than me. She was named after my grandmother on my mother's side. My parents had hoped for a boy and had planned to name him Benjamin after my grandfather on my mother's side. Instead they called me Betty. My sister and I were nicknamed Jetje and Betje, but for the most part I was 'Bep'.

Two years later, my brother Hartog Levie Lever was born on 4 September 1915. He was named after my grandfather on my father's side. We used to call him Harry.

I adored my little brother. He should have been a girl and I should have been a boy, because I always fought for him, even if it got me into trouble.

*Betty and her younger brother Hartog*

My father Levie Hartog Lever was born in Utrecht on the ninth of October 1874. He had six brothers and one sister. He moved to Amsterdam at age fourteen to work in the diamond industry as a cutter and polisher. He lived with an aunt and worked long hours. My father changed professions several times before eventually turning his hand to business and establishing two successful shops in Utrecht, which sold electrical goods.

My mother Floortje Lever-Woudhuijsen was born on the sixth of December 1885. She had three sisters and one brother. Her father died when she was quite young, and when her mother remarried she could not afford to look after her children. The three youngest children, including Floortje, were placed in a Jewish orphanage in Amsterdam. She remained there until age eighteen.

When I was a year old, we moved to Utrecht from Amsterdam. My father's family was quite orthodox, but we didn't attend synagogue very often. My father's shops on the Biltstraat and the Amsterdamsestraatweg were open on Saturdays.

Even if we didn't practise our faith, we *knew* we were Jewish. At Passover, for example, my mother would give us matzas with butter and brown sugar. She used to say they were *'boter dieven'* or 'butter thieves', because it took a lot of butter to make them palatable.

My father was a staunch Democratic Socialist and politically left-wing. He was very well read and our home was always full of books. He adored classical music and he fostered that appreciation in me. We used to attend concerts together.

My mother worked in the shop alongside my father, so we had a servant who would help with basic domestic duties. My sister and I also worked in one of our father's shops behind the counter. The shop was named Het Lampenkappenhuis, which means 'the lampshade shop'. I would have liked to go to university but at that time women were expected to just get married and have children.

My father and brother were both very active in the Jewish National Fund. Before the war, Harry had completed an agricultural course and planned to move to Palestine. He even had a ticket to go there, but it was a dangerous journey at that time and my mother couldn't bear to have her only son leave. On the day of his departure, she had a nervous breakdown and he didn't go.

I met Jacob Israel Fresco, or Jacques as he was known, in 1931, when I was eighteen years old. He was born in Utrecht on the twenty-fifth of August 1909 and was twenty-two years old when we met. I have always been very small and Jacques was much taller than I was, so my mother referred to him as the *langen*, or the 'tall one'.

The Fresco family lived nearby on the Voorstraat and also owned an electrical goods store. I was very fond of Jacques's father Abraham who was a business acquaintance of my father's. Although Jacques came from a merchant family, both he and his sister were very musical. In addition to working in the family business, he also played the piano at recitals.

His sister Esther, whom we all called Ellie, was a brilliant singer. She was born on the twenty-second of April 1916 in Utrecht. She was visually impaired and when she was a child the best eye doctor in Holland had given her an operation, which restored some of her sight, but she could not see very well.

We had a long courtship, which wasn't uncommon in those days, as it cost a lot of money to get married. My sister Jetje was engaged for ten years. I married Jacques on the eighteenth of August 1937 and we had a brief honeymoon in Belgium. When we returned to Utrecht, I moved to the Fresco home in the nearby Voorstraat.

The property had been in the Fresco family since 1903. It was a relatively large apartment. At first, there were five of us residing there, namely Jacques and I, his parents and his sister. Jacques's father Abraham died in 1938, and his mother died in 1941.

In August 1939, Jacques and I went on holiday to Scheveningen, which is a seaside resort not too far from Utrecht. By September, when war broke out, I had fallen pregnant.

On the seventeenth of April 1940 my only child, Abraham Jacques Fresco, was born. We affectionately referred to him as 'Appie'. It was three weeks before the

Nazis invaded Holland. When he was born, he weighed four pounds. The doctor held him up and laughed, saying, 'A good chicken weighs more.' He was so small that for the first few months of his life, I had to dress him in dolls' clothes.

It was a difficult time in the first years of my son's life. The Dutch army capitulated and the Nazis took control over Holland. In early 1942, all civilians were required to have an identity card. The Jews registered with the Joodse Raad (the Jewish Council) and identity cards labelled with a 'J' were issued.

We didn't think we had anything to hide. It didn't occur to us that we were being officially separated from the rest of the population. We never would have thought that the Nazis would want to murder us, just for being Jewish.

As the anti-Jewish laws were implemented gradually, we hardly noticed it. But then when a year passed, we began to see just how much life had changed. We were forbidden from riding bikes or using the tram. We also had a curfew.

My father used to take Appie in his pram to the park nearby and one day he came back looking exceptionally sad. He said that it was now forbidden for Jews to go to the park or sit on the bench.

We couldn't shop at non-Jewish stores, and there wasn't a great deal of food left in Jewish shops. Eventually they confiscated our businesses: my father's shops and the Fresco family shop. Officially, the Nazis 'paid' compensation, but this was a tiny percentage of their actual worth.

At first, it was only Jewish men who were called up for forced labour in the east, but then the elderly,

*Appie*

women and children were also required to report for forced labour. We suspected that something terrible was happening because once people left, they were never heard from again. Of course, we had no idea about the scale of the atrocities occurring in the concentration camps.

In August 1942, we went into hiding. Jacques, Appie and I went together, and Ellie went to a separate hiding place. She was caught and imprisoned before being sent to Auschwitz. She was murdered in the gas chambers on 22 October 1943, aged twenty-seven.

December 1942 was the last time I saw my father and my brother. They were hiding nearby where I was. Harry was looking after our father, as he was in his late sixties by then. I can't really recall how that meeting was arranged. I went to their hiding place, which was with a very kind family by the name of Haring. There were around six or seven Jews hiding there. My father

*Betty and her son Appie*

gave me a green and yellow scarf because I was cold.

When my father and brother were picked up, Harry had the address of where I was staying in his pocket. After that, Jacques and I separated because our hiding place had been compromised. We didn't have any money. We had been required to deposit our money into the Lippmann-Rosenthal bank, without having any chance to retrieve it. The Nazis had confiscated our possessions and the Fresco family shop, so it was very difficult to convince someone to hide me, especially with my two-year-old son.

Although the underground helped us secure another hiding place, it wasn't long before it was impossible to keep Appie with me. One time, the Nazis were near and he started to cry. I almost smothered him. I thought he would give us away, and then we'd have all been arrested.

In the end, the underground arranged for him to stay with an elderly couple who were devout Catholics. The couple believed that nobody would harm a child, but not too long after he arrived, somebody reported that there was a small child staying there and he was taken away by the Nazis and put into a crèche for Jewish children.

In the Netherlands, all the Jews were rounded up and processed at the Hollandsche Schouwburg, a theatre on the Plantage Middenlaan in Amsterdam. It was never designed to accommodate such large numbers of people. The conditions there were terrible, so in order to maintain order, the Nazis put all children under the age of twelve years in a crèche on the opposite side of the street. That's where they put Appie too.

A cousin of mine, Veronica Woudhuijsen, was born in Amsterdam on 29 March 1905. Her father Hijman was the only brother of my mother. She was employed by the Jewish Council as a social worker and additionally was a teacher at the Joodse Centrale voor Beroepsopleiding (JCB). She was working in the crèche and had connections to the resistance. Her objective was to save as many Jewish children as possible.

My son remained at the crèche for several months, and I believe that it was thanks to Veronica that he was later smuggled out by the resistance. Veronica was deported to Westerbork in late June 1943, and remained there for two months. She had a certificate to go to Palestine but as the validity of this could not be verified, she was sent to Auschwitz and gassed on 3 September 1943.

The Germans were waiting for me to give myself up, in order to send my son and me to our deaths. Children were not taken on transports unless they were with their parents so that the whole family could be processed together. By then, Jacques had already been rounded up and sent on transport to Westerbork. This was the place where Jews were held until they went on transport to the concentration camps in the east. I found out much later that he jumped from the train to Westerbork. These were ex-commuter trains rather than the cattle cars destined for the death camps, so it was relatively easy to escape. Jacques spent the remainder of the war hiding on a farm.

I wanted to be closer to Appie while he was held in the crèche, so I found a place to hide in the red-light district of Amsterdam. I remained there for around four months, until the resistance managed to smuggle him out and return him to me. It was very close to the Gestapo headquarters, and frequented by Nazi officers.

In order to blend in with the population, I bleached my hair and wore a small crucifix around my neck. I had obtained a false identity card from the underground and my name was Margriet van Loon. But as I officially didn't exist anymore, I no longer had a ration card.

The brothel where I was hiding was situated above a restaurant where there was a kind of cold storeroom built in. We used to prise up the floorboards and, using a hook, we would steal food. I remember we stole whole chickens, which was something because at that time meat was scarce. They never knew how the thieves went unnoticed, as the room was locked from the outside and heavily guarded. They didn't realise we were stealing the food from above.

I met Charles Niesten in Amsterdam. He was born in Haarlem on the thirty-first of August 1905. He worked as a furniture salesman. He later became involved in the Dutch resistance.

As I was in possession of false papers, I often went for walks in Amsterdam, passing where Appie was in the crèche on the Plantage Middenlaan and secretly visiting my aunt Grietje, who was living nearby. I also attended a series of Beethoven concerts conducted by Willem Mengelberg with Charles at the Concertgebouw. I often sat next to Nazi officers, which was dangerous considering I was Jewish, but my need to hear music was greater than my fear. Music was a temporary release from the terrible situation of the war.

By 1943, my parents, brother and sister had all been caught. My mother and Jetje had entrusted our household possessions to a maid who worked for us. She later turned them in to the Gestapo, in order to keep everything. My family were sent to Westerbork, and then on to different concentration camps. My parents and sister were sent on to Auschwitz.

My mother's younger sister Grietje Wouhuijsen-Droomer lived in Amsterdam with her husband Nathan and her youngest daughter Mary Rachel. Uncle Nathan worked as a shop assistant in a store that produced suits for Nazi officers. As his services were needed, the family was not called up until mid-1943. They were murdered at Sobibor on 28 May 1943.

My father wrote a postcard addressed to the Droomer family and threw it from the train to Auschwitz. It read: *Dear family, we are on transport. Tell it to others. We hope to come back. Levie, Floor and Jet.*

On the nineteenth of February 1943 they arrived at Auschwitz and were sent directly to the gas chambers.

My brother was sent to Kamp Vught in Hertogenbosch. He was able to send some letters from the camp to my aunt Grietje's family, and she passed them on to me. I kept them in my possession, even though it was quite dangerous.

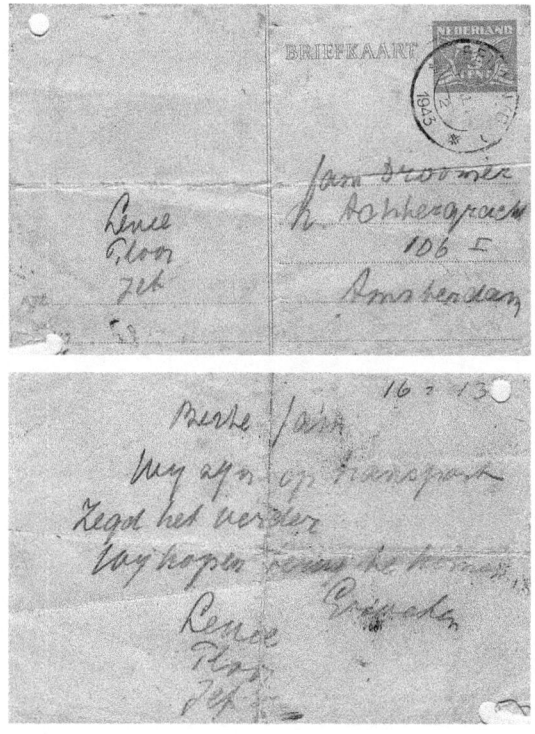

*The postcard that Betty's father tossed from the window of the cattle train transporting him, his wife and his daughter to Auschwitz*

My brother wanted vitamins, sugar, bread and condiments, and even sausage and liver. Before he was in the concentration camp he was a vegetarian. He also asked for warm clothing, towels and soap, saying that they had made him 'happier than these sort of possessions have ever meant to me.'

On the nineteenth of March 1943, he wrote that he was in good health: *Pass this message to all the family, also to Bep, from whom I received a package yesterday.*

*A letter written by Harry Lever while imprisoned at Kamp Vught*

*With your help surely I will hold on ... My dearest, sending you loving kisses. Think positively as I am.*

Not long after that, Harry was transferred to Sobibor, where he was murdered on the ninth of April 1943, at the age of twenty-seven.

In September 1943, Charles managed to find Appie and me a place to hide in the south of Holland, in the village of Lieshout in Brabant. We became part of a resistance group, and we stayed in a holiday home, which was owned by the Phillips electrical company. It was a summer home and not suited for the cold weather. The food in the countryside was better than in Amsterdam and we were able to get an egg or two from a farmer, and some milk.

On the grounds of the house where we were staying, our resistance group was hiding armaments and petrol for the cars they had stolen. We sheltered pilots who were shot down over Holland. There were British, Americans, and even Australian pilots. At night, we stole ration cards from the post office in Brabant. That meant there was extra food for the pilots, but some only stayed for a day or two, and we received their rations for the whole month. Some pilots remained with us for longer, depending on the state of their health. Before they left, we gave them civilian clothes. There was a little café there at the border: the back of the café was in Holland and the front was in Belgium. That's how they were smuggled across the border and on to safety.

I was in the village nearby where we were staying, running an errand. A German soldier stopped me and wanted to see my identity papers. I knew my identity card was false. He looked at me, then looked at my

*Charles Niesten with Betty and Appie with bleached hair*

photo on the paper and then looked at me again. My knees were like jelly because I thought he was about to arrest me. Then he smiled at me and asked, 'Have you got another photo like that? I'll send it to my mother and say you're my girlfriend.'

In August 1944, some members of our resistance group were captured by the Nazis. They had been found with armaments in their car. They were beaten until they informed the Germans where our group was based. A forester had seen them being arrested, and came to warn us that our hiding place had been compromised.

As the Germans came to the front of the building, I went out the back, with my son on the back of my bike. They were shouting for me to stop, and I heard gunshots, but I knew the surroundings there better than they did, and managed to escape.

The next month, in September 1944, the south of Holland was liberated. I always remember the sound of the Scottish pipers of the Canadian army playing, and knowing that at that moment, we were free.

Charles, who had been working with the Allied forces as an interpreter, returned to Brabant. When the German army capitulated, Charles was near Arnhem, where the peace treaty was signed. For his part in assisting the Allied pilots, he was honoured by the Air Chief Marshal of the Allied Expeditionary Forces, as well as by the General of the American army, Dwight Eisenhower.

After the liberation, the underground found two young German soldiers in the woods nearby and brought them to me. I had a small revolver given to me by the resistance, so that I could have shot myself if I was caught. I didn't want to be tortured and sent to a camp.

They told me I could shoot these soldiers as retribution for what the Germans had done to my family during the war. They were just boys, around seventeen or eighteen years old, and I thought of the fact that they had mothers too. It simply wasn't in my nature to take away someone's life. They were arrested and taken into custody.

We were very fortunate to be in the liberated part of Holland during the *Hongerwinter* (the 'hunger winter') in 1944–45. There was a blockade on supplies and millions of people were starving.

After the war, Charles found a place for us to live in the Hague. I desperately tried to locate my family and the Red Cross was of little help. As the months passed, I began to learn that my immediate family – my parents, sister and brother – as well as many uncles, aunts and cousins, had all been murdered. I didn't know it then, but Holland had the highest Jewish death toll of any western European country.

The shock of the tragedy had turned my hair white overnight. I was only thirty-two years old and completely alone in the world, except for my son. If I hadn't had Appie to look after, I don't think I could have gone on.

I saw Jacques after the war, but we had been separated for several years by this stage. He had met another woman and I had Charles, so we decided to divorce and marry our respective partners. I married Charles on 29 October 1947.

Jacques married Elisabeth Leeuwin on 29 July 1947, and they had two children: Isidore (Ido) born on 27 March 1949, and Margaretha Rachel (Marion) born on 13 May 1953.

Life in Holland after the war was very difficult. There had been extensive damage to infrastructure and housing was in shortage. My parents had a home in Bilthoven, but during the war there had been tenants in the property, and after the war they did not want to leave. When the tenants vacated the property in Bilthoven, we moved there, in 1947. It was a very nice neighbourhood and had conditions been better, we would have stayed. Unemployment was high and Charles found it difficult to obtain work. Some of our neighbours were emigrating to Australia and we decided to leave Holland too.

Originally I wanted to go to Israel, but there was a great deal of demand at that time as there were so many displaced Jews still in camps in Europe. As Charles was not Jewish, I thought it better to go to either Canada or Australia. I wasn't so keen on the cold weather, so when he tossed a coin in order to make the decision, I was happy to move to Australia. We applied to move there and were accepted in 1950.

We arrived at the port in Fremantle, Western Australia, on 21 March 1951. Perth was such a primitive city in those days that if I could have crawled back to Holland I would have done so. As building supplies were scarce at that time, we took a prefabricated house and a caravan with us on the ship. Within a year, however, the combination of the hot climate and the white ants destroyed both the house and the caravan. We also brought a car with us, but it was ruined after driving on the country roads, which were like corrugated iron.

Charles began to work at the Midland brick factory not long after we arrived in Australia. In the 1960s he worked as a taxi driver but eventually I became the breadwinner. I worked as a receptionist in a physiotherapy clinic on St Georges Terrace in Perth. I was employed full-time for the next twelve years, and I never took a single day off work.

*Betty and Charles Niesten in Perth*

When we came to Australia, Appie became known as Albert and took his stepfather's surname. As we spoke Dutch at home, he only learnt English when he went to school. The first time I heard him speaking English was in a school play.

My son worked a variety of jobs, including as an ambulance driver for St John Ambulance and as an orderly in a hospital. He spent many years travelling. In 1966 he moved to New Zealand and worked for the post office and from 1973–74 he lived on a kibbutz in Israel.

In 1974 he met Robyn Finley at a Jewish singles night in Perth and they both made aliyah to Israel the following year. They decided to come back to Australia to start their family and were married on 14 November 1976.

My first grandchild, Rafael Hartog, was born on 27 May 1978. His middle name was to honour the memory of my brother Hartog. Two years later, Leon David came along on 19 May 1980. My only granddaughter, Jessica Hilda Fleur, was born on 1 June 1982. The name Fleur was in honour of my mother Floortje.

Having grandchildren has been a wonderful experience for me, because it was the first time in almost forty years that I had family again. As such, I have always been exceptionally close to them. My grandchildren visit me every week and we telephone each other regularly.

The Nazis wanted to murder all the Jews in Europe. I have never forgotten the terrible years of the war and all that we endured, but I have survived. I have made it my mission to tell my story to as many people as possible, so that the innocent lives which were taken were not in vain. If we can educate the next generation, then we may prevent such atrocities from taking place again in the future.

*This text was written by Betty's granddaughter Jessica Niesten, based on extensive interviews. Betty passed away in May 2014, aged 101 years.*

*Portrait of Betty's family painted by her granddaughter Jessica Niesten, reconstructed from surviving photographs*

## Isaac (Henk) Piller

My name is Isaac Piller and I was born on 10 December 1932 in Amsterdam, to Reintje and Mozes Piller. I was their second child and eldest son. I had an older sister, Betje, and after me came Esther, Benjamin, Hartog and Judith. My baby brother Ronald was born later, in June 1943.

We lived in the eastern district of Amsterdam, in a row of houses that all looked the same. We lived on the first floor, and I can remember the layout of our home well enough to draw a map of it. I shared a bedroom with my brothers, Benjamin and Hartog. It wasn't a big house, but I have fond memories of my time there.

My early childhood was a happy one. My family was loving and affectionate. I was particularly attached to my mother who was warm and kind and had a lovely voice. She was always singing. My father worked in a bakery that specialised in making matzas for Passover. Ours was a traditional Jewish home and I can recall pleasant Friday nights with the candles lit for a special meal. We celebrated all the Jewish festivals with our large extended family. I don't speak Hebrew, although we learned some at school, but I still find myself remembering many of the songs and prayers when I hear them. We often visited our grandparents on both sides, who were very loving, always ready with lots of kisses and cuddles. My mother's parents had a diamond and gold shop and my grandmother would always give me a cent to buy something sweet with. The money came from a pocket in her petticoat. We were surrounded by aunts and uncles, so I grew up in a close and loving family. These memories are still clear and strong in my mind.

I attended a Jewish school with my sister, Betje. I was happy there, and did well at my schoolwork. I enjoyed learning. On freezing cold days my mother would come to meet us at school, bringing socks with her to put over our shoes so that we would not slip and fall on the ice on the way home. She was a caring and protective woman. Our lives were those of a normal family in Amsterdam. The children in the neighbourhood all played together in the street. I didn't feel any different to my friends.

In May 1940 Germany invaded Holland. I can remember hearing the planes flying overhead, but I had no idea what the war would change for me and my family. Everyone was saying 'this is war', but I was too young to understand.

One day, while I was playing innocently with a friend in our street, his father came up and slapped me.

He said, 'Stay away from my son, you little Jew.' I was shocked by his anger; I had done nothing wrong and I didn't understand. This was my first experience of being made to feel different. I was so upset I ran to my parents. They consoled me but they could do nothing about it for fear of reprisal.

A few weeks after this incident my pet cat Spotty was killed. His mangled body was left on our front doorstep. We were all distressed and unable to understand how anyone could be so cruel to a helpless animal. Again, my parents couldn't say or do anything. We were Jews and they were terrified that worse would come for us.

The Jewish people were becoming more and more isolated. We were made to wear the yellow Star of David to show we were Jews and set us apart. Jews weren't allowed on the trams, trains or buses. The parks even had signs stating: 'NO ENTRY TO DOGS AND JEWS'. We became the target of cruel taunts and ridicule.

Food was rationed in Holland during the war, and we were not given coupons. We lived close to a baker's shop and sometimes my mother sent me to get bread. Often I was taken out of the queue because I was wearing the Star of David. I couldn't understand why I was being pushed out of line. Sometimes the woman in the shop took pity on me and gave me a loaf of bread. My father was still working and helping other Jewish people to store their belongings with neighbours or friends. For that he was paid in food, which he brought home to us.

The corner shop near where we lived was owned by an old Jewish man. I was there when it was vandalised and looted. I saw the old man getting bashed and he called out to me to run home, for my own safety.

The round-up of Jewish people began in the middle of March 1942. Teachers and children were taken from the Jewish schools. If their parents went to collect them, they were also taken away. Our school was closed and my education stopped. I was only nine years old. Most people were initially taken to the concentration camp at Westerbork, in the province of Drenthe near the German border.

Holland had been a traditionally tolerant country before the war. The Germans knew this and they formed a very strong Dutch Nazi party to help them with their 'work'. From this time on, fear ruled every day of our lives.

I have vivid and terrifying memories of loud boots coming up the stairs to our door on the first floor. The Germans came up the stairs in groups of four or five to collect Jews from their homes. As the eldest boy in the family, I was the one who had to open the door. My parents would quickly duck into bed and I would tell the soldiers that they were very sick. The Germans were afraid of contagious illness and so they kicked me and told me they would return soon. We had to keep our little siblings quiet. I can still see the fear in my parents' eyes every time they heard German boots on the stairs. These memories still haunt me.

Early each morning my father would slip out of the flat to check up on family members who lived nearby. If he returned with bad news about some of our extended family it made us even more fearful and apprehensive. My parents were particularly concerned about their parents. One day my father returned with news that his parents had been taken by the Nazis. His mother, who was partially blind, had been pushed down the stairs and hurt. My grandparents were sent separately to the Sobibor where they were gassed on the thirtieth of April 1943.

Our home became our prison. There was no school, no entertainment and very little to do. Our radio had been confiscated and we had to be quiet at all times. There was no heating and no one outside was brave enough to supply us with coal or anything that we could burn. It was terribly cold and we all suffered. We were not allowed to go outside or look out from the windows. There was very little food and we were always hungry. I never saw my mother eat. I think she gave her share to the children. With six children at home, I don't know how she managed with the washing, for it could not be hung outside and with no heating it would have been impossible to dry.

I remember that my mother would sit us down on the lounge, all in a row, and sing to us. She had hand gestures that went with the songs and we would join in. She sang in Hebrew, Yiddish and Dutch. I still remember many of the songs she taught us and my wife Wilma often catches me singing them. One of the songs I remember was called 'Under Mum's Umbrella'.

My mother was pregnant, and when she went into labour we had to stay with our neighbours on the ground floor. She gave birth to my baby brother in our small flat on the sixteenth of June 1943. There was no one to help her and no medical care. The rest of us didn't even know what was happening. They named him Ronald. He was the only one of us not given a Jewish name, and the only boy not circumcised, as there were no rabbis left to perform the ceremony.

Daily we heard stories of whole families who had committed suicide by gassing themselves in their kitchens. My parents contacted the Dutch underground and through them met a man called Johannes Bogaard. He agreed to find families willing to take the children and hide us from the Germans. The first time Bogaard came he took Ronald, who was only six weeks old, and Judith, who was two and a half. My parents were absolutely beside themselves and could not stop hugging and kissing their little daughter and newborn son until this man, whom they did not know, took them away.

Bogaard was a tall, fierce looking man. He was serious and always in a hurry and we children were very afraid of him. We did not know why he took our siblings away. When they left our home we were all grief-stricken. The crying was terrible. We were not allowed to know where they were going and we were afraid we would never see them again. We heard no news of them at all.

About a week later Bogaard returned. This time he took Hartog and Benjamin. Again we wept bitterly, the separation of our family was heart-wrenching. We did not know if they were going to safety or to their deaths. We heard so much talk of death.

Two or three weeks later Bogaard came back for Esther and Betje. I will never forget the screams of my parents as they stood against the wall and saw their beloved children taken from them. Each parting was traumatic. Now I was the only child left.

Not long after, a neighbour contacted us and said I was to go with my parents to his place early in the morning. He lived at the end of the street. Before we'd even walked a hundred metres people were in our home, dragging out our possessions like scavengers. They took clothes, furniture, anything they could find. These people were our neighbours, whose children I had played with.

When we arrived at our neighbour's house we were told to stay on the first floor. Two days later Bogaard returned for me, the last of the children. I was ten years old and I did not want to leave my parents. I made a fuss but they talked to me and cuddled me and my mother said, 'It will be all right, we'll be together again on your birthday.' I could not take anything with me but my mother gave me a little eraser and said, 'You keep that, it's a lucky one.' I still have it to this day. Then she said to me, 'Go with this man and don't look back.' Of course I couldn't help but turn around. That was my last memory of my dear parents, they were crying uncontrollably, for now all seven of their children were gone.

Bogaard told me not to speak. He gave me an apple, which I ate ravenously in a couple of bites. We took a bus and again I was told not to speak, but to look straight ahead. I didn't know where we were going, everything was unfamiliar and strange. He took me to a young married couple. The woman did not want to risk having me, but was talked into it by the men. I remember very little about that first night. I felt alone, unwanted and very frightened. I slept little and cried a lot.

The following morning Bogaard returned. He told me to choose a new name, and I chose Henk. I'm not sure why, it was the first thing that came to mind. To this day I still call myself Henk, and not Isaac, the name my parents gave me. Wherever I stayed after that I was given a new surname, something related to the family I was staying with so they could pass me off as a relative. I always kept the same first name, however. I was always Henk.

I was taken to a place in the country about four kilometres from Amsterdam. It was along a dyke, near a river. There were farms but it was too small to be called a village. There I stayed with John Korsman and his wife. They had three children – two girls who were about my age and a boy who was younger. John was kind to me, but his wife didn't want me there. She said nasty things and made me do chores. I was only given old clothes to wear. I remember she gave me an old pair of shoes and the heels were worn down. I couldn't walk properly in them but she said it was because I was a Jew, because my ancestors had walked in the desert. I was always trying to behave and be helpful. I couldn't understand why she didn't like me.

*Henk with the Korsman children*

It was the same everywhere I stayed; the men were always kinder to me than the women. This was very hard for me as my mother had been so warm and affectionate. I craved that motherly love. It has taken me many years, but I can now see how frightened these women must have been. They were protective of their own children and I was a risk that could put their family in danger. However, that was impossible for a ten-year-old boy to understand.

John Korsman's father had a farm and a little Jewish girl called Naomi was hiding there. She told me she was the same age as me, but I later found out she was only nine years old. On my second visit there they took us to a big shed and made us each dig a hole in the ground. The hole had to be big enough to hide in. We practised hiding in these holes, with straw and old bags to cover us. One day the Germans came in their trucks

*Naomi*

and we had to hide in these holes. I was scared but I stayed quiet. However, Naomi started crying and they found her. Once they'd found her they stopped looking. I waited in the hole for someone to come and get me, afraid the Germans would come back. It felt like days before John came to let me out. This incident scared me so much I was unable to speak for some time.

After this frightening experience it was no longer safe for me to stay with the Korsmans. I was told they would find a new family to hide me with, but until that time I would have to stay in the attic. I was hidden there for six weeks. There were no stairs leading to the attic, just a hole in the ceiling, so a ladder had to be brought to get in or out. It was a small dark space with no windows and I couldn't stand up. I could hear the children playing outside, but there was nothing I could do and the days seemed endless. I started to count the bricks in the wall, some of them were slanted so they were half bricks. I added them all up, the full bricks and the half bricks. I had always been good at maths. I did this every day, and even now I can't have exposed bricks in my house or I start to count them. I was allowed out of the attic only once a day in the evening to go to the toilet, and the woman brought me a little food. I was so miserable in that place, I wanted to die.

While I was in the attic it was my mother's birthday, November twenty-eighth. I'd only been to school for about one and a half years before the war, so I couldn't write very well. I asked John to write a letter for me on her birthday. I felt sure I would hear back from her, but I waited in vain. I asked if he'd received any letter back from her but he told me he had not. I probably asked again the next day. It was very disappointing for me, as

I longed for news of my family, but I didn't know how bad things were at that time.

Finally, I was called down from the attic. I had been in that dark and cramped space for weeks and it had taken its toll. My eyes were badly affected by the darkness and I had trouble adjusting to the daylight. My body was unnaturally bloated from malnutrition and lack of exercise.

Outside there was a woman waiting to take me to the next place I would be hidden. She was riding a pushbike and had her son with her. I rode on the back of the bicycle and it was such a relief to be outside in the fresh air again. They took me a long way to a small village called Hoofddorp.

The woman was called Betty Geerlings and I was to stay with her and her husband Fred and their four children – one daughter and three sons. The children were all around my age, some a few years older or younger. They must have been worried one of their children would say something about me at school. It was always a great risk for the families that hid me.

The Geerlings family was Catholic, and I went to church with them every Sunday. I didn't like going to church and I didn't understand their ways. The first night I ate dinner with the family they said grace and I automatically put my hand on my head in place of a yarmulke. I was told never to do that again, but sometimes I found my hand creeping up subconsciously!

One Sunday, while walking to church, I saw my sister Betje. I wasn't aware that she was living so close to me. I wasn't allowed to speak to her or acknowledge her presence but it gave me hope to know she was alive. I was never asked about my family and there was no way

*Fred and Betty Geerlings*

to find out where they were or how they were doing. I felt very alone and that one glimpse of my sister was a great comfort.

My eleventh birthday was on the tenth of December, soon after I went to live with the Geerlings family. I did not tell anyone that it was my birthday, because I believed my mother would come to get me as she had promised. I was very upset and thought she did not want me anymore. I imagined that all my family were at home and that they'd forgotten about me. On that birthday I just went to bed and cried. I did not want to celebrate my birthday ever again. I'm in my seventies now and I still do not celebrate my birthday.

The Geerlings family lived in a two-storey house and they made me a hiding place in the top of one of the cupboards between the two floors. It was very narrow and cramped. Fortunately I only had to get into this space when people came to visit the family. I was never made to hide there for an extended time. I had to be very quiet and it was impossible to move in the tiny space. I had to practise getting in and out of this hiding space many times. On the weekends I was sent to various members of the Geerlings' extended family for safety. I dreaded this as I felt unwanted and unwelcome at some of these places.

One night Fred Geerlings woke me up suddenly and told me that I had to run quickly and hide in a field of wheat, some hundred metres from the house. There were Germans in the street and they were shooting. Fred said to me, 'Sit down and hide there, don't worry, I'll come to get you.' It was so cold and I was in my pyjamas and had bare feet. I heard trucks coming, they went into every home to look for people who were hiding, not only Jews but young men who had been called to work in Germany. It was so cold in the field and I was soaking wet and shivering. I was tall enough to look over the wheat and I kept bobbing up to look even though I'd been told to stay down.

Finally, after a couple of hours, Fred came to collect me, and I cried with relief. He said to me, 'Don't worry, sometimes I cry too.' I couldn't believe that this big, tough man ever cried and it made me feel a bit better. I still have nightmares about running and hiding in the field. The chill I caught that night has given me long-term lung problems.

While I was living with the Geerlings family, our neighbours threatened to betray them. The Germans were offering money to those who turned in Jews. When Fred heard about this he was so angry he went over to confront them. He said that if they turned me in, they would live to regret it. They must have believed him, as I was never found.

Fred was always very kind to me but Betty, like the other women I stayed with, offered me none of the affection I was used to from my own mother. At night, I would go with the children to say goodnight to their parents and they would hug and kiss each of them, but not me. I was not fully included in the family or treated like one of their own.

At the very end of the war I had a chance to see my baby brother Ronald. I think I overheard some visitors tell the family that he was living about four kilometres away, and so I borrowed a bike from the youngest Geerlings boy and rode there. Initially the woman who was looking after Ronald did not want to let me see him. I had to plead with her and explain that I was his brother and eventually she let me in. Ronald was only two years old and he didn't know who I was, but we played together and he didn't want me to leave. I went back once more to see him. I just wanted to see him. I felt responsible for my little brother.

They weren't as strict about keeping me hidden at Hoofddorp and sometimes I was allowed outside. One day, early in 1945, I was playing with some children and I won a game. The boy I had been playing with said, 'You will never see your mother and father again.' He was being spiteful but this shocked and upset me.

When the war ended there was dancing in the streets. People threw big parties and let off fireworks, whatever they could find. Everyone felt the pressure lifted. I wanted to go straight back to my parents but no one said anything about it. I had to wait a long time to find out what happened to my family.

Both my parents had been taken to Auschwitz. My

*Mozes Piller with all seven children after the war*

mother had been gassed there on the nineteenth of November 1943, not long after her thirty-third birthday. My father survived, but it was six months before he came out of hospital. He had lost both of his feet and was not well enough to care for his children. I lost close to one hundred and fifty members of my extended family during the Holocaust, but miraculously all my siblings survived. We all met up when my father came out of hospital. It had been two and a half years since we'd seen each other.

Homes had to be found for all of us. Ronald was adopted by the family who had looked after him since he was a few weeks old. Betje was fifteen years old by then, and got a job working as a housekeeper for a doctor. She worked seven days a week and the labour was hard. All she got for this was her room and keep. Judith was taken in by a family friend and Esther and Hartog went to an orphanage about forty kilometres away in

Hilversum. Benjamin went to a different orphanage, one that used to be a prison and was nearly a hundred kilometres away from Amsterdam. There were only so many children that each orphanage could take, which is why they were separated.

I remained with the Geerlings family. They told me I was allowed to stay with them only if I agreed to become a Roman Catholic. My father was not very happy about this, but I really had no choice. I was only twelve years old and the Geerlings had been so good to me that I felt I had to stay with them. I travelled a long way to visit my brothers, but they weren't happy to see me, they used to think, 'Here comes the little Catholic boy.' They didn't understand at the time. I was not close to the Geerlings boys, but I had my own friends. We started a band together and I played the guitar.

I was able to go back to school after the war. I'd lost three and a half years of my education and it was very hard to catch up. I had been in grade two before the war, and they put me in grade four when I went back. There was a kind teacher who stayed back at night to help me catch up and with his help I was able to progress to grade six at the same time as the other children my age. This teacher came to the house and tried to encourage Fred and Betty to send me to university. He said I was bright and had a lot of potential. I wanted to go because both my friends from the band were going to university. However, the Geerlings' own boys couldn't go, so they didn't want to put me ahead of their own children. Instead we all went to a trade school. I learnt carpentry and cabinetmaking because I didn't want to get my hands dirty. I studied drawing because I wanted to become an architect but I didn't get the chance.

After four years of school I had to join the army – it was compulsory. I was in the army for eighteen months, but they must have known something about my experiences as they did not give me a weapon or make me do any shooting. It was never mentioned that I was a Jew. Instead I learnt about the radar.

I came to Australia when I was twenty-one, with two of the Geerlings children. Fred and Betty came three months later. I arrived in Perth on 1 February 1954 at the Fremantle docks. I was supposed to be meeting someone who would take me to a job in York, but I ended up staying at a boarding house with lots of other Dutch immigrants, not all of them legal. Initially I didn't want to come to Australia, because my family were still in Holland. We kept in touch by post, because it was too expensive to make long-distance calls.

I practised carpentry, but it wasn't for me so I went to work in a grain mill in Cannington. After a few years I became the manager there. After that I became a general manager in an anodising shop for aluminium in Belmont.

I met Wilma in 1954, at the end of the year. The owners of the boarding house knew Wilma's parents. I went to pick them up for a New Year's party and Wilma was there. I asked if she was coming to the party too. She said no, she was a nurse and had duties that night. I talked her into cancelling her work and coming along. I had a motorbike and I offered her a ride the next day. After I got to know Wilma, I decided to stay in Perth. We were married in 1956. We had three children – two girls and then a boy. They're all well and healthy and have their

*Piller family reunion in the Netherlands*

own children. We now have eight grandchildren and five great-grandchildren. I'm proud and happy that my family is doing well, and all have had the chance to go to university and be successful in their careers.

I have stayed in contact with the Geerlings family and have had them recognised with Yad Vashem as Righteous Among the Nations. When we took the children to Holland we visited the Geerlings and they treated our kids as their own grandchildren. I have been back to Holland six times. The first time I went back my brothers were upset with me for leaving the family, but I explained to them that I felt I had to go with the Geerlings family. It took them a few years, but they have come to understand this.

The man who found hiding places for me and all my brothers and sisters, Johannes Bogaard, was also recognised by Yad Vashem for his bravery and sacrifice.

*Henk and Wilma*

During the war he worked tirelessly to save Jews, hiding up to seventy people on the family farm and working with the Dutch underground to find other hiding places for other Jews. Several of his family members were imprisoned and murdered by the Nazis as punishment for their support of the Jews. Bogaard and his family helped around two hundred Jews to survive the Holocaust.

Looking back on my life I'm very fortunate to have left Holland because my brothers and sisters are still strongly affected by their experiences during the war. One of my brothers is still illiterate as he missed his schooling. Esther and Hartog had some education at the orphanage, but they didn't get proper schooling. We were all affected by the horrors of the war, but also by missing such a vital part of our education.

I have had a good life in Perth, even though I came here with nothing and had to work for everything I have. I'm retired now, and have enjoyed playing golf until recently and volunteering for Princess Margaret Children's Hospital. I've volunteered with them for seven years. Sometimes I talk about my experiences during the war with groups of school children. This was very hard for me to do at first, but has become easier over the years.

My gratitude goes to my parents for their unselfish act in handing us over so that we had a chance to survive. It must have been terribly hard for them, but they would be proud to see all their beautiful family, grandchildren, great-grandchildren and great-great-grandchildren.

## *Fryda Grynberg*

I was born in 1920. I was the eldest child in a family of five siblings. We lived in a small town in Poland called Rutki-Kossaki. My father was a bootmaker and life for us was very hard. What I mean by a hard life is that when I used to come home from school, my mother had arranged a list of chores for me to do. After school I never had time to go and play with other children or even do my homework. I had to walk two kilometres for water because we didn't have plumbing in our house. Some people did have these luxuries, but I came from a family that was not extremely poor, but was not rich enough to have plumbing. Our house did not have carpets so we also had to help our mother to scrub the floor. Of course we also didn't have washing machines and we had to do this by hand. So my parents arranged a full half-day's work for me to do this.

I also had to learn to speak, read and write Yiddish, which is the language that the Jewish people used at that time. I also had to learn our bible. I was not a jealous type of person, but I was envious of the children playing in the garden and even eating snacks like an apple. For us it was different. You watched every bite your brothers and sisters had and when you left the table you still felt hungry.

When my mother arranged work for us, it had to be done. We could not complain. Before I turned fourteen, my parents wanted me to be self-supporting so they sent me to a lady to learn a trade – dressmaking. You had to pay to be an apprentice, but these people took me in to see what I could do. When they saw how well I could sew they even bought me some presents occasionally. I was very fortunate that they really liked me and so that is how I became a dressmaker.

When I turned fourteen, my parents decided that I had to go to the bigger city of Bialystok, which was fifty kilometres away, as there wasn't much work in our little town. My home town, Rutki-Kossaki, only had one hundred and fifty families whereas Bialystok had sixty thousand Jews. You can imagine how I felt as only a fourteen-year-old, sent to this big city. At night I couldn't sleep and cried to see my parents and be with my family. It was impossible to visit them as I could only travel by horse and carriage and it would have taken a whole night to get home. There were no cars at that time. We did write to each other and it was good that I had learnt to read and write in Yiddish.

I got married in 1938 at the age of eighteen to Mendel Rosenbaum, a factory worker, and by the time war broke out in 1939 I had already had a baby daughter named Genia. Bialystok was located in the eastern part of Poland occupied by Russia. We heard rumours of cruel and barbaric acts in the German-occupied western part but we had no way of confirming them.

When the Germans invaded Bialystok in June 1941, all the Jews were forced into a ghetto. This was located in an old part of the city. It was surrounded by a wall. Movement in and out of the ghetto was possible only through a single gate, which was controlled by German guards. Only certain workers were allowed out and they had to go to specific factories each day. All Jews were required to wear Stars of David on their clothing to identify them readily.

No food was provided by the Germans. The Ghetto Council, or Judenrat, used its meagre funds to purchase food for distribution to people in the ghetto. Most people survived by using money or valuables they had brought with them into the ghetto to buy food that had been smuggled in. There was far too little food to go around. Hunger became a way of life. There were no newspapers or radios. I soon lost track of time as one season blended into the next.

Sometime in 1942 my sister arrived at the ghetto. She told me that the rest of our family had been killed. Afterwards she returned to Rutki-Kossaki. I never saw her again.

Early in 1943 the Germans began clearing out the Bialystok ghetto. They were transporting the Jews in cattle trains, to be carted off to Treblinka to be disposed of. They would come to the Ghetto Council and demand that a certain number of Jews be supplied for transportation. If their quotas were not met they would seize people from the streets at random. We learned to stay hidden whenever these round-ups were taking place. The people who went on these transports were never seen again. Their clothing would turn up outside the ghetto from time to time, being worn by non-Jews. People who were allowed out of the ghetto during the day would often comment after seeing a familiar article of clothing that had belonged to a family member or friend.

My husband and I were finally caught in one of the round-ups. Together with our baby daughter, we were jammed into a cattle wagon and transported westwards. We had to stand up all the time. There was no room to move. We went for days without food or water. Occasionally a loaf of bread was thrown into the cattle truck. When this occurred there was a surge of people fighting over it. There were no toilet facilities.

The first major stop on this route was the death camp Treblinka. By now we had reached the inescapable conclusion that we were all going to be killed. My husband and I decided to try and escape. I strapped my baby onto his back and as we approached Treblinka, when the train slowed down and the doors were unbolted and slowly opened, my husband jumped from the train onto the railway tracks. At that moment, a train passed travelling in the opposite direction and they were both killed. When I saw what had happened I fainted and fell to the floor of the wagon.

Other people had also jumped from the train. German guards stationed in the woods beside the tracks saw what was going on and opened fire with machine guns. They sprayed the wagon with bullets and there were people dying all around me. Many bodies fell on top of me and I was lucky to have survived. The train finally stopped at the Treblinka station and I could hear the carriages at the rear being uncoupled.

The train journey continued for several more days and we finally stopped at a concentration camp called Blizyn. The Nazis dragged us out of the wagons and shaved our heads and we were put to work. We wore ordinary clothing. I worked in a factory sewing uniforms for German soldiers. Each morning we received a drink of hot water and two ounces of bread. This had to last us all day. In the evening we were given a cup of watery soup. On the rare occasions that we found a piece of potato the size of a one-cent piece in our soup we would joke about it and pretend that the soup was beautiful and thick.

The camp was surrounded by a barbed wire fence. There were several watchtowers outside from which we were watched all the time. We slept on wooden boards in barracks also made of wood. There were no mattresses or blankets. We were crammed in, many people to a bunk. Men and women were kept separately. During the day we all worked together in factories as slave labourers. No talking was allowed.

Every morning and every night we had to assemble and be counted. One morning a young boy of about ten didn't wake up in time. As punishment we were all made to kneel down on the ground, which was covered with gravel, and keep our hands above our heads for many hours. When the missing boy was finally found he was stripped and beaten shockingly in front of us.

When the Germans wanted some fun or

entertainment when they were drunk in the middle of the night, they would wake us, screaming in German 'All Jews out!' As we hurried from our barracks, confused and still half-asleep, the Germans would beat us with rubber batons for their amusement. And so that is how the days and the nights passed.

In the spring of 1944 we were transferred to Auschwitz. On arrival, the number 15698 was tattooed on my left arm. I was issued a standard uniform of a long striped dress. There was no underclothing. The camp was surrounded by electrified barbed wire fences and men and women were kept separate. No contact was possible.

Once a day, we were forced to strip naked and an inspection was carried out. Those who appeared unfit were taken away. We never saw them again. At one stage I developed a serious infection in my right hand and it became very swollen. I was terrified that I would be declared unfit. Two Jewish girls who had some authority in my barracks arranged for the abscess to be lanced. This was done without any anaesthetic and not by a doctor, but by a vet. The two girls covered for my absence from rollcall by pretending that I was doing a job for them and this allowed me to recover. Had the Germans realised what was happening, all three of us would most certainly have been included in the daily selection.

In summer we were kept in the wooden barracks day and night. We were permitted to go to the toilet only once a day. This was a large room with many holes in the ground. There was no privacy. In winter we were forced to walk many kilometres in the rain and snow, wearing only our flimsy uniforms, to dig holes with shovels. We never knew what the holes were being used for or even if they were being used for anything at all. One hundred and twenty girls would set out in the morning and only one hundred would return at night. The others died of hunger and cold and fell to the ground exhausted, unable to walk any further. The guards would set their Alsatian dogs on them to kill them quicker and make death easier for them.

The women's barracks were situated in a part of the camp I now know to have been Birkenau. It was adjacent to the gas chambers and crematoria. On the way to work each morning and on the way back each night we could see large numbers of people being taken to the gas chambers. We could also sometimes see them through cracks in the walls of our barracks. Many of the people were well dressed. On the way some of them screamed and cried and the noise was very frightening and terrible. Others sang, probably because they thought that they were going to be freed. During the gassing the noise was terrible. After a while it became silent. This went on non-stop for twenty-four hours a day. The ovens worked day and night, burning the bodies of those who had been gassed. The smell was unbearable.

Many people became so depressed and frightened that they ran to the electric fences to kill themselves. Some committed suicide by cutting their wrists with glass because they couldn't take it anymore.

After about ten months, I was taken to Bergen-Belsen. Here there were no ovens, just piles of dead bodies lying on top of each other waiting to be burned. We were housed in a large barracks with a sandy floor. There were no bunks. We were so weak that all we could do was to crouch down next to each other on the floor. It was very crowded and there were no toilet facilities. People relieved themselves where they crouched. Those who still had their senses covered it with sand. We were too weak to move. When a person next to you died, we thanked God that we had someone to lean on.

Only those who could still walk a bit received a cup of soup once a day. Some would bring soup in a cup to feed the very weak with a mouthful. Some prisoners ate enormous lice that were crawling on their bodies. Some would even eat the dead bodies. To us life had no meaning. All we wanted to know was that Hitler had lost the war.

When we heard bombs falling around us, we gathered up our last energy and crawled out on our hands and knees and prayed that the bombs would fall on us and end our misery. Soon we noticed that there were no German soldiers around us and no one was guarding the soup. Those who had strength took some soup, but soon found that they were sick because the Germans had poisoned it before they ran away. Many died straight away, but I only had a mouthful and was just sick.

When the Allied soldiers finally arrived in May 1945, we were transferred to the quarters previously used by the German guards. Our stomachs were pumped out and we were also sprayed for lice. I don't know the nationality of the liberating troops and I was too weak to really care. I only remember that they wore khaki uniforms with a cap and spoke a language I couldn't understand. In the end only a handful of us survived.

I was very sick when I was liberated and decided that I wanted to go back to Bialystok to see if I could find my family. Unfortunately there was no one. A few Jewish people gave me food and looked after me.

Back in Bialystok I met and married my second husband, Sol Grynberg. One day a man from Melbourne named Mr Wise, who was born in Bialystok and whose family was killed, decided to help other survivors. He wrote offering help to emigrate to Australia. We applied and he arranged all the paperwork. It took us about two years to get to Australia. We went to France and stayed in Paris for a year in a refugee camp, waiting for transportation. The French government provided three meals a day for us. Being pregnant, I was one of the first survivors to leave Europe.

On arrival in Fremantle, some of the Jewish community came down to meet us and hear all about the war in Europe. I discovered that I had a cousin here and we were persuaded to get off the ship and settle in

*Fryda after the war*

Perth as they would help my husband get a job. I had my baby two months after arriving in Perth and could not go to school to learn English. It was also more important to work and make money to survive. My husband worked day and night to make a living. I did not feel that there was any anti-Semitism in Australia, but life was very hard and the government did nothing to help the refugees. We did not know the language and had no clothing or furniture, no handouts. Hard work is the only thing that saved us. I think that I survived the war due to having to work hard as a child, having no servants and also not having much food and therefore learning to eat very little as a young growing girl. I have never returned to Poland and actually feel it was a mistake to go there after the war as it was too upsetting. The only good thing was meeting my husband there.

Every day when I wake up I open my eyes and thank God. Then I say, 'The sun is shining for me.'

§

Fryda and Sol arrived in Perth in 1948 after a long sea voyage from France on a ship named the *Partizanka*. Their son Peter was born shortly after their arrival, and a second son, Max, was born seven years later in 1955. Apart from each other and their children, Fryda and Sol were alone in the world. Both had lost their entire family during the war, they had limited contacts in Perth and did not speak the language of their new homeland. Sol had spent the war in the Red Army, conscripted by the Russians when they invaded Poland, and he had his own troubling memories and losses to contend with.

Like so many of the refugees streaming out of Europe, Fryda and Sol were taken in by another Jewish

*Fryda and Sol on their wedding day*

family, renting a room until they were able to afford their own lodgings. Sol had trained as a tailor in Poland and, with Fryda's talents as a seamstress, the couple soon began taking in sewing work to pay the bills. Sol eventually found more lucrative work in wool buying and established a successful business, often travelling to farms in Northam and York.

Eventually the Grynbergs bought a home in North Perth. Fryda's sons remember her delight when the mortgage of their first home was paid off, her celebration of the stability and safety of owning a home after all that she had lost. Fryda and Sol eventually saved enough money to buy a block of land on Armadale Crescent in Mount Lawley, where they built a new home for their family.

Fryda and Sol became involved in Yiddish theatre soon after their arrival in Perth and participated in a wide range of concerts and productions over the years, embracing the emerging Jewish dramatic scene with

*Fryda and Sol*

great energy and enjoyment. In 1980, the General Secretary of Maccabi WA, a Jewish community organisation, wrote to the Grynbergs to thank them for their assistance in providing the Jewish people of Perth with 'a memorable, nostalgic reminder of our background'.

Fryda was also an incredibly talented cook and poured all her passion and love into feeding her family and friends. Her traditional Yiddish dishes were famous, with people clamouring to place orders for gefilte fish and begging for copies of her recipes, which she had written out by hand in Yiddish. She would bake towering cakes of all varieties and sublime kreplach, often cooking multiple different dishes for family gatherings to ensure that each person had their favourite dish.

Fryda did not speak much to her family about her early life in Poland or her experiences during the Holocaust; they were different universes, the old

> But it was your live talk which convinced me it was all true.
> Your courageous talk proved to me that everything I had learnt was actually right.
> You are the proof that everyone must know about.
> When I heard you telling the tale of your life I was wondering where you dug up enough courage to talk about these horrific times.
> We all appreciate you giving up your time to send the truth to us about the treatment of the World War II victims.
> Keep up your great strength because every child that hears your story will experience the overwhelming feeling that you create.
> Thankyou for talking to us and we hope you will manage to overcome the vivid memories of the past.
>
> Yours Sincerely

*School student's letter to Fryda*

separated from the new by a kind of fissure in time itself. Like so many survivors, she had made a determined effort to turn back to the world, to look only forward. However, the memories of her wartime experience continued to erupt into her new life and to shadow the safety and contentment she had found in Australia. 'I am like a rotten apple – fine on the outside but inside not so good,' Fryda once explained to a journalist from *The West Australian* newspaper.

At night the past broke through in the form of terrifying nightmares and Fryda would sometimes wake up with dark bruises where she had clutched her arms in fear during her sleep. The terror and torment of the war years manifested themselves in her ever-present fear for the safety of her family, her anxiety when her husband was not with her and her ceaseless worrying over her children. In every house

*Fryda and family*

she lived, her chair was always turned to the window so that she could watch the street for the safe return of her husband and sons from work or school. If her husband was delayed at work or her sons were late coming home from school, Fryda would be stricken with terror, calling all the local hospitals to ask if they had been admitted. As they grew older, Fryda's sons better understood this constant vigilance: she clung too closely to them because she had seen her first child killed horribly in front of her, she loved them so fiercely because she had lost everyone else.

This same impassioned love, though with less of the overwhelming anxiety, was lavished upon her grandchildren, whom she adored and spent as much time with as she could.

When the Holocaust Institute was established in Perth in 1990, Fryda agreed to volunteer as a speaker, sharing her story with the many groups of students and other visitors who came to the Institute over the years. She became a regular speaker, telling her story again and again.

Fryda received hundreds of letters from students who had come to listen to her speak about her experiences. She kept every single card and letter and carried them with her in a black briefcase. They became a kind of tangible symbol that her words had been heard and received, that something of what she had suffered, as incomprehensible as it would always be, had been communicated and understood. As tormenting as it was to continually describe the terrible details of her wartime experiences, it also gave Fryda a measure of solace. In some way a legacy was being created, her memories placed into the hands of another generation. 'It was your live talk which convinced me that it was all true,' one student wrote to Fryda. 'Your courageous talk proved to me that everything I had learnt was actually right. You are the proof that everyone must know about.' Providing the students who came to the Holocaust Institute with this profound, living sense of the human realities of the history they were studying was vitally important to Fryda.

Fryda also recorded her testimony for the Survivors of the Shoah Visual History Foundation. In 1997 she received a letter from the foundation chairman Steven Spielberg commending her for her strength and generosity in sharing her story. 'Far into the future,' Spielberg wrote, 'people will be able to see a face, hear a voice and observe a life so that they may listen and learn and always remember.'

Fryda died in 2002, on her eighty-second birthday.

# Bill Glatzer

My name is Bill Glatzer and I was born in December 1927 in a small town called Horodenka. It was situated in the Ukraine, on the border of Poland and Rumania, and had a population of approximately sixteen thousand people, of whom around three to three and a half thousand were Jewish. I was the oldest of three children and the only boy.

My father had a bakery in the town. We all worked there, and we lived above the bakery. I can remember delivering bread and rolls to the shops in baskets early in the morning before school. I used to envy the other boys, who were warm asleep in bed while I walked to the shops. In winter the temperature would drop to as low as minus twenty-eight degrees.

I went to the school in Horodenka and a lot of the

children in my class were Jewish. There was some anti-Semitism, and sometimes I got into fights with the Ukrainian and Polish boys, defending myself and other Jewish children.

War broke out in September 1939 when I was not quite twelve years old, and in my final primary grade. Soon after the war began, the Russians came into our town. We had heard that the Germans were already in the western part of the country and the Russians took over the area in which we lived. They 'nationalised' my father's bakery and put him in as the manager. Our family still lived in our home above the bakery. At first I still worked in the bakery, but when things settled down I returned to school for the next grade. Now I no longer had to get up early and deliver bread and I had time to play sport. I was good at sport and enjoyed athletics, soccer and skiing.

At the end of June 1941 our lives were completely changed. We heard that the Germans were attacking Russia and the Russians left our town. The Germans invaded and occupied Horodenka. At first only a few German army police came in, and the Ukrainian police in the town worked with them.

Very soon afterwards we were forced to leave our homes and move into the ghetto, which was established in the Jewish part of town. All Jews had to leave their homes and move into the ghetto. As Horodenka was a central town surrounded by tiny villages, the Jews from these villages were also moved to live in the ghetto and this swelled our numbers to close to four thousand people. The ghetto had no walls but it was surrounded by a barbed wire fence. There were armed guards at the main gate, but security was not very strict because the town was not large and we had no way of escaping from there. We all had to wear the Jewish star on armbands on our clothing to readily distinguish us. The ghetto was situated less than two kilometres from where we had lived and when we moved there we took what we could carry from our home. We were crowded into one room – my grandmother, my parents, my two sisters and myself. We had no furniture and we slept on the floor.

All property was confiscated, and my father and I were forced to work in the bakery which he had once owned.

At this time most of our personal property was also confiscated, including our fur-lined winter coats, our radios, bicycles and skis. The clothing and bicycles were taken for the use of the German army, and they confiscated the radios to cut our contact with the outside world. I can remember breaking my skis because I was determined that the Germans would not get them. New orders and restrictions on our lives seemed to come out almost every day.

There was a Judenrat, or committee of Jews who were supposed to represent us, but they had no power and just passed the orders down to us from the Germans.

The Jews of Horodenka had smaller rations than other people and all we had to eat was bread. If people had money or clothes which they could exchange, they could sometimes buy vegetables from the farmers who lived close to the ghetto. We needed passes to get in and out of the ghetto and so only the people who worked outside the ghetto could get the extra food.

The first *aktion* came in December 1941. All Jews were rounded up and we had to go to the local synagogue. Almost the whole Jewish community was taken to the

Siemakowce forest, a few kilometres from town. They were all shot, including my grandmother, my mother and my two young sisters.

This *aktion* took three days in all to complete, for they had only three trucks to transport a very large number of people and it was midwinter which made for a slow journey. Two of the truck drivers were Poles and they warned the people that they were being killed and to run away. This was very difficult but many people tried to hide and were often caught and killed later, especially when they were exposed trying to find food.

About five hundred Jews were still needed to work in the essential services in the town. My father and I were included in a small number of 'useful' Jews who were still needed to work in the town. For example, most of the engineers and the workers in the electricity station were Jewish, and were needed to help run the town's power supplies. The town had a sugar refinery and flour mills and some Jews also worked there.

The ghetto was made much smaller and we continued to work in the bakery. Our rations were barely enough to live on and working in the bakery helped us to survive. We used to hide bread for ourselves and for other people in the bottom of a bin under the coal, which we needed for our fires. When we were searched on our way back to the ghetto, the guards saw only the coal on top of the bread.

The second *aktion* came in April 1942. The SS rounded up more Jews for shooting, and we were at work outside the ghetto when this happened. They took all the Jews they could find in the streets. We went on working in the bakery until September 1942, when the remaining Jews from Horodenka had to assemble in the town square for what they called 'registration'.

*Bill's sisters killed in Siemakowce forest,
Beppi (left) and Sarah*

My father was released, but I was taken with most of the others to the Kolomyja Ghetto, in a bigger town, about forty kilometres away. When we were rounded up some of the people tried to escape by running away, but they were shot and killed on the spot.

In October 1942 I escaped from the Kolomyja Ghetto. I had volunteered to work for the occupying military police, and I got to know a soldier there, who was a driver. At this time I was not yet fifteen years of age. He had to go to Horodenka, and he suggested that if I could get together ten to twelve people, he would take us back there, for a fee. I collected the people together, but had no money myself. He took me for free because all the others paid.

The soldier had to pass a checkpoint at a little town on the way and he explained that if the guard on duty was a friend of his then we would be allowed through, but if he was someone he did not know, the truck would be searched and that would be the end of us. Fortunately for us, the guard on duty was one of his friends.

While I was in the Kolomyja Ghetto, I heard that the authorities had transferred my father to another bakery on the outskirts of town, so I was the first person dropped off, on the edge of town. I was very afraid of being discovered and hid in the outside toilet. By sheer luck my father came in and I told him how I had escaped.

At this time he had a room in the bakery. The Polish people managing the bakery were good people and told my father that I could hide in the attic for a short while. Unfortunately I developed typhoid fever and I became very ill. One Jewish doctor had been retained in the town because he was so useful in the hospital, which now catered almost exclusively for the military. He agreed to come and see me in the attic at night, and he brought the necessary medicines for my illness.

The man from the bakery overheard him telling my father that I was highly contagious and that many people in the town could become infected. So he gave me twenty-four hours to leave and find somewhere else to hide.

There was a Ukrainian boy called Nick working in the bakery. He had been at school with me, and he offered to take me home to his place – a brave and dangerous thing to do. The small house had a family bedroom above the stove in the kitchen, for warmth in the long winter, and I shared Nick's bed. His sister had a Ukrainian policeman as a boyfriend and one night they were downstairs when he heard me coughing. Nick called out that he had a bit of a cold, and this saved me. I stayed there for about two weeks until I was better.

Then the Germans began rounding up young people for forced labour in Germany. Nick's mother told me to hide in the potato pit, which was outside the back of the house, until the round-up was over. Then my father found a place for me to hide. This was with a Polish family and I stayed in the cellar for a month, when my father joined me because he was no longer safe from the Germans in the bakery.

The man in this particular Polish family remembered how my father had been kind to him and given him work in the bakery early in the war, after he had lost his job when the Russians occupied the town. He was glad to help us, although we were penniless. The family fed us for another month until just before Christmas.

The house we stayed in was divided into two, and the family in the other half of the building had internal quarrels and called the police to sort things out. It was no longer safe for us to remain there and we had to leave suddenly on Christmas Eve. I will never forget that morning. A blizzard was blowing and it was freezing cold.

We had almost given up hope of survival in the snow when my father remembered a little railway bridge not far away, with a wide drain underneath it. We climbed into the drain, which was about one metre in diameter. It became covered with snow at both ends, and we were then protected from the wind and the worst of the cold. In the evening we dug our way out and crept back to the house. We looked through the window and saw a policeman sitting inside. My father decided to go back to the home of the manager of the bakery which had once been our own.

He promised to hide us in the cellar of the bakery, where we made a bunker. We did this by digging a hole in the earth underneath the cellar. It was about a metre deep and we could not stand up in it. We spent almost all the time in the bunker. When the workers were not there we could go into the cellar. We never saw daylight or had a chance to breathe fresh air. There was one boy already hiding there – he sometimes helped in the bakery when the other workers were not there. I was shocked by his wild appearance when we first got there – he looked like a hunted animal. We were fed by the wife of the worker who lived in the bakery and we stayed there until March, when the weather began to improve. We were in the bunker in hiding almost all of the time and life was very uncomfortable. We had no clothes to change and no facilities to wash or keep clean. We had lice and fleas.

It was becoming too dangerous to remain there and we heard about a cave which was a few kilometres from town on the edge of the forest. We went there one dark night. It had a narrow entrance and went eighteen to twenty metres underground then it opened out into a narrow cave with a high ceiling. We lived deep in the cave, about two hundred metres from the entrance. There were a few others hiding there too – about a dozen of us altogether. It was so narrow that we each found our own sleeping space away from the others. We hid there from March 1943 until April 1944, when the town was liberated by the Russian army.

Survival in the cave depended at first on food, which was left for us by the manager of the bakery. When the vegetable crops grew in the surrounding fields, we raided them for food to survive. The cave was on surrendered farming land and a German army officer managed the farm. Some of the people hiding in the cave had worked on the estate and he knew that they were there and helped them with food. He returned home on leave and when he did so he left us with a couple of rifles. When we went out to seek food we had the rifles with us and when the farmers would not help us, we took what we needed. Sometimes they thought we were Partisans when they saw the rifles and they just gave us what we needed without question.

Although I was barely seventeen, I later joined the Russian army and I was there for nearly two years. I fought on the Third White Russian Front in Prussia. After the war finished in May 1945, we went to Manchuria to fight the Japanese. In Manchuria I learned a little English from the American troops who were stationed there.

After the war was over I was free to go back to Poland, where my father was waiting for me. He arranged for

*Bill in uniform, 1945*

*Bill after the war in Paris*

papers to come to Australia. We lived in Paris for about a year while we waited to get passage on a ship to this country. In the time there I went the Berlitz School, where they teach languages, and learned English.

We came to Australia in 1948 and my father, who had helped me to survive, died in 1970. I have lived here ever since.

§

Bill and his father arrived in Melbourne in 1948, where he lived until 1954. In Australia, Bill was able to engage once again in his love of sports. He enjoyed snow skiing in the mountains of Victoria, took up water skiing and was involved with the Maccabi Senior Soccer Club in Western Australia. It was through his love for sports that Bill met his first wife Leah at the Maccabiah Games – often know as the 'Jewish Olympics'.

*Bill with Leah, Ben and Hanya in Perth*

Leah's family were from Perth and Bill gave up his tickets to the Melbourne Olympics in 1956 to stay in Perth and get married. A year after their marriage, Bill and Leah bought the Oxford Milk Bar, which was attached to the Oxford Cinema in Leederville, and ran the business together. In 1961 Bill began working in partnership with Leah's brother in a cabinetmaking firm in Yokine. Bill had no previous training in carpentry, but had always been good with his hands and learnt on the job. The firm was called Ultra Furnishers and they specialised in bedroom and household furniture. He continued to work in the firm until 1985 when he retired.

Bill and Leah had two children – a daughter, Hanya, born in 1957 and a son, Ben, born in 1959. He was very open with them from a young age, educating them about the war and his experiences during the Holocaust. He wanted to make sure that his children understood and

*Former central synagogue of Horodenka*

would never forget the atrocities that had occurred in Europe. At the time, there were few records of survivors' stories, and so it was up to the families to keep these memories alive.

Leah passed away in 1970. In 1973 Bill married again. His second wife Janina had no children and became Ben's and Hanya's stepmother. Family was very important to Bill, having lost all but two of his extended family during the war. Only his father and an uncle survived, and Bill's children grew up without relatives on their father's side.

Bill made many friends, both in Melbourne and Perth, who had been through the war in Europe and had similar experiences. He stayed in contact with them throughout his life. After his retirement, he worked very closely with the Orthodox Jewish community in Perth, helping to resettle Jewish immigrants from South Africa, Russia and Zimbabwe. He spoke to groups of school children through the Holocaust Institute and

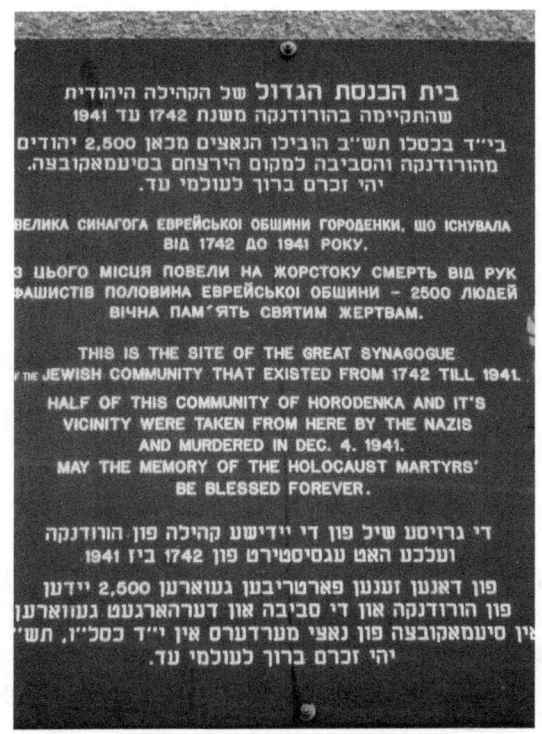

*A commemorative plaque at the site of
the Great Synagogue of Horodenka*

his story was recorded by the Survivors of the Shoah Visual History Foundation.

Bill never went back to Europe, but many years later his first grandchild Jeremy returned to Horodenka to visit the places where Bill lived and was hidden during the war. Jeremy found that a plaque had been placed in the Jewish cemetery to commemorate the Jewish people who had been murdered in the war, including Bill's stepmother, grandmother and two sisters.

The trials and losses that Bill and his father

*Bill with his first grandson Jeremy, 1982*

endured during the Holocaust affected him every day of his life. He is remembered as a loving and fair father, as brave yet humble, and as an inspiration to his children and grandchildren. Bill passed away on 14 March 2006.

*Bill with his children Ben and Hanya*

*Bill with all of his grandchildren in Queensland, 2001*

## *Rosalie Rothschild*

I was born in 1919 in the Netherlands, in Breda – a relatively small town in the southern province of North Brabant. My father's family were resident in the area. When I was six I moved to Kampen, an even smaller town in the province of Overijssel, fairly close to the German border. Here it was that my sister, my brother and I grew up.

My mother's family had lived there for over a century. They lived in a very old house with gables and my mother was born in that very house. My mother used to tell us many stories of the goings-on in this house, which later became a warehouse, housing the carpets and mats of my father's and grandfather's trade.

Their wholesale carpet business was well known and my family were well respected in Kampen. We had

*Rosalie's house before the war*

a happy childhood and family life there. We grew up in this out-of-the-way town, almost oblivious to the fact that we were Jewish. There were perhaps eight Jewish families in the town, the remainder being church-going Christians. It was a quiet place, noted mainly for the farmers who viewed it as a centre. It was surrounded by meadows and farmland. The nearest town was Zwolle, a train ride away. We attended the local government schools, and in the main, were untroubled by anti-Semitism.

Two minor incidents remain in my memory. My mother and sister wore spectacles and on one occasion I heard someone speak of us as the 'Brillejoden' – Jews who wore spectacles. It did not seem as though they were being derogatory, so we ignored the remark. On another occasion, I recall my grandfather being called 'Mattenjood' – the Jew who deals in mats. The farmers gave him the nickname on account of his trading in plaited mats. However, these farmers were his friends and again, no more was thought of it.

Our youth in Kampen was very happy and we had many good friends. Despite this happiness, times were changing across the border in Germany. Our parents became concerned. Being so close to the border they thought it wiser to move westwards. In 1938 we settled in the little village of Overveen in the municipality of Bloemendaal, very close to the city of Haarlem.

The news filtering out of Germany was most worrying. The way in which the Jews were being treated was of grave concern. My grandparents, who had themselves left Kampen and were now living in Arnhem, welcomed relatives en route out of Germany. Yet, though Germany was our neighbour, somehow we felt secure. We felt that nothing could happen to us in Holland, certainly not in the far west of the country. Perhaps the border areas would give cause for concern, and in 1939 my grandparents were persuaded to come to Overveen, where we found them a lovely little cottage.

Life somehow went on. In 1939 I went to England to work as an au pair in Chelmsford in Essex. Even there the signs of the coming danger were in evidence; trenches and shelters were being prepared. Despite this, an optimism of sorts prevailed.

When Germany made its move in March 1939, I was hastily called back home. Perhaps there was fear of war between Britain and Germany, but Holland would surely be out of it. Indeed, my parents laughed when I told of the worrying thoughts of many I had met in

England. 'There will be no war involving Holland,' they said. How wrong they were.

We lived peacefully in Overveen until the tenth of May 1940, when the Nazis invaded Holland. We were woken at 6 am by my father who said, 'Girls, do you hear that noise? Those are German bombers and they have invaded our country.' Later we heard bombs landing in the neighbourhood; we heard aerial dogfights. The danger of war was upon us.

The actual days of the war were terrifying. We experienced the horrific bombing of Rotterdam, which you could hear even in Overveen. Against the strength of the German air force, backed up by their army, Holland had no chance. The war, as it involved a response by Dutch forces, was over in five days.

In those five days I experienced at first hand the reality of war. The aerial dogfights, the overflights, the bombing – all spelled danger. On the third day of the war my parents decided it would be better for my sister and I to leave Holland. The chosen route was from Ijmuiden, the seaport situated west of Amsterdam at the mouth of the North Sea Canal. We knew there were boats travelling from Ijmuiden to England.

We never got to Ijmuiden. While we were en route we saw the Shell oil refineries go up in flame. It was like an inferno on the outskirts of Amsterdam. Then we saw the traffic. Hundreds and hundreds of cars were on the same road, travelling bumper to bumper at virtually no speed at all. It was utterly depressing and unbearable. It gradually dawned on us that we may not even reach Ijmuiden, and that even if we did, we may not be able to sail. We talked it over and decided it was better to return. We managed to escape from the endless stream of traffic and made our way back to Overveen. I will never forget the looks on the faces of my mother and grandparents.

This was but the beginning. For the moment we continued life as normally as was possible. However, even five days of war can change things. The German occupation brought the biggest change. The Germans had taken possession of the large buildings and were everywhere.

At this time I was working as a pharmacist in Zandvoort, a holiday resort some ten minutes' train ride from Overveen. The pharmacy belonged to a Dr Tichelaar, a well-known doctor in the area. A very humane and kind man, he embraced me when I returned to work after those five days, saying, 'Everything will be all right, nothing is going to change, you have nothing to worry about.' However, right there in Zandvoort one could see the German soldiers marching in the streets, singing their songs. It sickened me.

So occupation took hold and Holland began to feel the pressure. The Germans were very clever in developing their plans and only brought in their laws gradually. In 1941 came the first changes, with the introduction of identity cards. We had to go to the town hall where a fingerprint was made of our right index finger. A 'J' was added to the card of every Jew.

Then Jews had to hand in any gold or diamonds, and soon afterwards their radios as well. This was probably in response to our finding out what appeared to be on Hitler's agenda as regards to us Jews. We did our best to live as normally as possible, though rumours began to abound. We were particularly concerned by the rumour that Jews may no longer work for non-Jews. It was also feared that we may have to leave our homes.

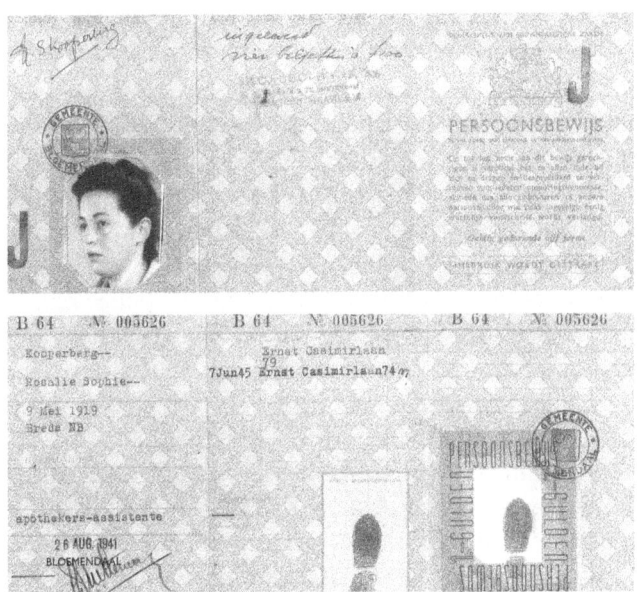

*Both sides of Rosalie's identity card, issued in 1941, bearing a 'J'*

At this time my sister was a secretary working in the post office in Haarlem and my brother was in high school. We were fortunate in that we had a number of good friends in the non-Jewish community. An uncle of our best friend, Nel, took our jewellery and some important family papers for safekeeping. This was perhaps the first sign of our family's determination to try as far as possible to avoid fulfilling the decrees that were being enforced. Of course this brought with it added danger as, if our friends were implicated, there would be severe punishments for all involved. It soon became obvious that within the Dutch population there were collaborators. Organised into a party called the NSB, they worked as a fifth column within the country, though a number were dealt with at war's end.

1941 brought many changes. Soon those dreaded laws requiring Jews to leave the employ of non-Jews became a reality. My sister became a nurse in the NIZ – the Dutch Jewish hospital. I continued to work in the pharmacy until the spring of 1942, when I was officially forced to stop.

My grandparents were friendly with a policeman in Overveen. Early in 1942 this man came to tell them that the rumours about having to leave our homes were true. Also, about this time my father received a letter from the Gestapo saying he had to report to their office in Amsterdam. My mother went with him, though waited in the area in the hope this was just a visit to their office and nothing more. I did not go to the pharmacy that day.

My parents returned later that day. Apparently my father had waited all day to be seen. In the end he was told it had been a mistake and he could return home. The combination of these events brought a realisation of the extreme dangers of the times.

Our friendly policeman called again to tell us that expulsions from our homes were certain to occur in March 1942. Now was the time to place those items of sentimental or other value in safekeeping. If the expulsions were to occur, then it seemed clear that we would be forced to live in a ghetto in Amsterdam. My parents commenced looking for alternative arrangements. Ghettoes could mean only a repetition of what had been occurring in Germany; bringing the Jews together and deporting them.

At about the same time as I left the pharmacy, we got a notice that we had to leave our house. On the thirty-first of March our house was sealed. I remember the Germans sealing our door. We went on the electric train to Amsterdam. As we sat in the train – Mother, Father, my brother and I (my sister was at work in the Jewish hospital) – I noticed sitting near us a lady with whom I had been working in the pharmacy in Zandvoort. She looked at me, and tears just poured out of her eyes. I do not know whether she realised that we were at the start of what was to have been a deportation. She just stared and cried.

We were taken to somewhere in Amsterdam. We were required to undress, given a health check and were allowed to get dressed again. I still remember the feeling of deep humiliation first to be in that train surrounded by our luggage, and then the undressing. However, we had little time to reflect on that, for at this moment we made our first move against our occupiers. We went not to the planned abode, but to a rented apartment in Amsterdam South. Mother had indeed heeded our policeman friend's warning and had rented the place some months earlier.

That brought with it other problems. As we were living in an area forbidden to us Jews, I decided I had to do something about my black hair. It was easy for me to obtain some peroxide. I took a bottle home and applied it to my hair. It was very painful, stinging. I put some towels around my hair and hoped for the best. Next morning I could not believe how I had changed. I was blonde, my dark brown hair gone. My parents, who did not know of my plans, were aghast when they first saw me. However, once I had explained to them that it would be safer, especially on trips to the Jewish area, their upset abated. This subterfuge was to help me in time to come.

*Rosalie with bleached hair in 1942*

We lived in the flat in Amsterdam South from the thirty-first of March to early September. We had to be extremely careful. Of course we did not wear our Stars of David – a risk in itself, as we were required to do so. I managed to get a job in a pharmacy, the Rembrandt pharmacy, owned by a Mr Rosenbaum. Though officially registered on 20 July, I had been working there from March. In Amsterdam there were a few pharmacies which were designated as only being open to Jews, these of course being in the Jewish area.

Travelling to and from the Jewish area brought its own difficulties. I travelled daily to the ghetto by bicycle. I would enter the Jewish area through a very narrow lane. Then I would put on my Star of David. Of course, I did the reverse every night, always checking that there was nobody watching me. I was lucky for, in over five months, I was never caught.

Now the Germans embarked on a policy of calling

up families who had to leave Holland. In the pharmacy I had to make up parcels for people who were leaving for Germany. Included in these parcels were medicines which might be needed. I remember how depressing this work was, knowing that perhaps one day the parcel would be for ourselves or for those we knew.

Within Holland the laws became more stringent. It now became dangerous for Jews to meet with non-Jews. However, my mother managed to keep up some contact with her best friends and through them my parents made contact with the Dutch resistance movement, known to us as the underground.

It was through the underground that my mother was able to obtain false identity documents. We all realised that something had to be done, for we as a family were flirting with terrible danger through our twilight existence in an area where we were actually forbidden.

The times were tense. We had to leave our flat and went for a time to my mother's sister, who was herself also living in a forbidden zone. My aunt had a shelter and when there were rumours of a round-up, we hid there. The shelter was cleverly made, but it still gave me the shivers when we had to use it.

*Rosalie's certificate of proof of work in the pharmacy*

We were preparing to take on our false identities. Mine was to be in the name of Frouwke Braaksma. The identity document of this Frouwke Braaksma mentioned a scar on the left thumb. I became concerned lest this be checked once I had taken on this identity. I went to a friend, a recently qualified doctor, and asked him to give me a cut on my left thumb. He asked what it was for but I refused to tell him. After receiving this deep cut and having had it duly stitched and bandaged, I went home in pain to be confronted again by astonished parents. They were impressed at the lengths I was to go to to assume my false identity. Hiding seemed not too far off, but reality struck in September 1942.

On a certain September morning, I entered the old Jewish quarter of Amsterdam and made my way as usual to the Nieuwe Herengracht and to Mr Rosenbaum's pharmacy. The streets seemed too quiet. I entered the pharmacy. Only one other staff member arrived. Nobody else came, not even the owner. That was unusual in itself, for he was always early. Something had to be wrong.

Suddenly there were strange noises; screams, screeching of cars, much shouting of German soldiers. It then dawned on us that a *razzia*, a raid, was taking place right there. We locked the pharmacy and considered what would be the best thing to do. My friend was very nervous and wanted to get away, but I persuaded her to stay as she was surely safer indoors than on the street. We looked for a hiding place in the pharmacy. There were very large windows containing the normal shopfront displays. Underneath the displays were cupboards into which we put items not needed for display just then. We opened these containers and saw there was ample space for the two of us. We climbed in and waited, knowing we had little choice. There were no curtains to protect us and even the door was partly of glass.

The noise increased. We lay there in fear. The soldiers came closer still, now almost upon the pharmacy. We could hear the Gestapo and the soldiers knocking on the doors and demanding people come out of their houses. Then they came to the pharmacy. I heard one say in German, 'Would there be anyone inside?' The other replied, 'No, there are no people in there, the place is empty and closed.' They tried to open the door, but left once they realised it was locked. We lay absolutely still, petrified.

Exhausted and afraid, we waited. Then we heard the telephone ring. My colleague refused to answer it, but I decided the risk was worth taking. There had to be a reason there was a call now, and why the telephone kept on ringing. I cautiously walked to the telephone and answered. A voice responded, 'This is the Red Cross.' They were checking if there was anybody in the pharmacy. We were told we would be saved. We had to unlock the door but remain in our hiding place until they came. They said they would come by ambulance and soon we heard a car draw up. They had with them a stretcher, on which each of us in turn was placed, covered by a blanket, seeming as though we were ill. We were told we would have to go through a German roadblock, where the ambulance would be checked, so we would have to appear as though we were very ill. The Red Cross workers told us there had been raids all over. They had been very busy.

We were duly stopped by the Germans. They came into the ambulance, but we kept our eyes closed. We probably looked tired enough to be ill after our ordeal.

As I understood German, I knew what was being said. Somehow luck was with us and we were allowed to proceed. We came to a safe area, from where we were delivered to our homes. My colleague stayed the night, but went home the next day. I was never to see her again; she perished.

For us, the relief at my surviving this raid was but a spur to move quickly towards finding a safe refuge. We made contact with the resistance, to go, as we said, 'underground'. The first to be hidden, to go 'underground' – or in Dutch: *'ondergedoken'* – was my brother. I was the second to go, then my sister and finally my parents. My sister, my brother and I were hidden in separate places, but my parents remained together.

We were well prepared for our move. I had a small suitcase with just enough clothes for a few days. We had all done our homework, learning our new names. Sometimes mother would ask unexpectedly, 'Who are you? Where were you born?' I felt confident I was no longer Rosalie Sophie Kooperberg, but Frouwke Braaksma. Braaksma was a Frisian name, native to the most northerly province Friesland. Frouwke is also a typical Frisian name, meaning 'little woman'. With my blonde hair and new identity, I was ready.

There was still the goodbye. I will never forget it, as I did not know whether I would see my parents again. I remember wanting to be brave. Father stayed at home, but mother came, saying, 'I want to walk a little way with you.'

I had to go to Amsterdam Central Station. There, after meeting the underground contact, who would be wearing a flower in her buttonhole, I would leave Amsterdam for my new destination. Mother and I walked to the tram.

We said goodbye without a tear, it was not allowed. I was suddenly alone, not even able to look back.

When I entered the tram I got a shock. There were so many Germans in that tram, German soldiers. I thought, 'How am I going to do it? I know I am blonde, do not look particularly Jewish, but ...' I had my identity card and I knew I wanted to survive. Whatever happened I would do my best not to fall into their hands. I remember some of the soldiers staring at me, but I arrived at the station untroubled.

I found my contact sitting on a bench. She had already purchased my ticket and told me to go to the correct platform. It was the train to Rotterdam. She would travel in the train but not in the same compartment. When the train reached Leiden I was to go to the exit, past the ticket collector, and she would catch up with me then. It seemed as though it was some spy novel. I was terrified but tried to appear calm.

Although I remember so much and so clearly the happenings at that time, I cannot remember how I came from the station to the address of my hiding place. I do remember it was not too far from the station. It seemed to be a very big house near a park. On entry, my contact said, 'Frouwke, you are going to live here and you are to do exactly what the people want you to do. They will tell you where you are allowed to go. Try to relax and you are not to worry about a thing. I will see that things will be as good as possible. Should something go wrong, you will be told what to do. All I can tell you about myself is that my name is Fiet.' With that, she kissed me, told me again not to worry about my family, and she was gone.

So started my period of underground existence. I was with a family of three small girls. The parents of the lady of the house were also there. The man who lived there was Huib, his wife was called Liz. These kind people were also well educated. I was to live in the attic. Only if it were safe was I to come among the family.

My life changed overnight. I had to get used to keeping myself occupied. That, in itself, would be difficult. I was taught to spin wool, which was used to make mittens and similar things to be used by the underground, especially for the soldiers. I began studying, reading a lot, and made use of my hands by knitting. Being what was effectively a prisoner was very difficult. The recent dangers had been difficult, but at least I had been busy. Now time lay heavy on my hands. I had time to think about my family and to wonder how they were getting on.

New Year's Eve came. We gathered in the living room. First we played some charades and were about to partake of the food when Huib heard a noise near the front door. We looked at each other. Huib went to the door and returned with the blood drained from his face. He told us that an envelope had been slipped under the door, in which a large sum of money was being demanded. The blackmail note stated that the sum had to be delivered at a certain spot and time, otherwise Huib would be reported for harbouring a Jewess.

The happy gathering was over. I had to prepare to escape. Liz told me to get dressed as warmly as possible. Huib did likewise. Liz brought us to the other side of the attic, where there was a small window. It faced the neighbour's attic window. Apparently Huib was able, by previous arrangement, to open the neighbour's window. However, there was a narrow space between the two houses. I said it was impossible for me to cross that divide. I guessed Huib could, as he had long legs, but I was very short. To this day I do not know how I did it, but despite the fear of falling three storeys, I made it. The memory of that crossing is with me still.

Huib told me to wait until he had been down to see the people who were living there. He told me that the owner was a parson, a female deaconess, and that she knew Huib worked for the resistance. After a few minutes he returned to fetch me. As I followed him downstairs he told me that there was a party taking place downstairs. As I came into their dining room, everyone stopped and stared. Some told me not to worry, that they were all friends of Huib, and that a solution and a safe passage would be found.

The parson and her friends decided they would leave the house in pairs, chatting and acting as though they had just come out of a party. One of the guests would walk with Huib and one with me. Huib had emergency addresses for both himself and for me. The person walking with me would walk me to my refuge. It was freezing and snow lay fairly well set on the ground, but otherwise it was a still night.

My 'partner' was of course the parson, this woman of God. As we walked she spoke of my need for trust, for she felt sure I would survive. That walk and her words that cold night were like warmth to my inner spirit, warmth and support that I still recall now.

I was in my second refuge for one night. However, it too remains etched in my memory. I was exhausted, close to collapse. My new host and hostess tried to calm me down. They told me not to worry, another plan would be worked out for me. I asked whether I could do the washing-up as I needed to do something to unwind. I began, but was in such a state that I broke one glass after another. Gradually I got myself together and did the whole job.

My third abode was at the home of Mrs van Campen, a member of a well-known Dutch publishing house. She was a very fine lady, most kind to me. She was on her own. The situation was ideal, but the times were not. Mrs van Campen had heard there would be raids in that part of Leiden and it was wiser for me to leave before it was too late. Within a week I was again on the move.

My guide, as on two of the previous occasions, was Fiet. Yet this was to be the last time I would see her. Fiet van Gilsen was the half-Jewish daughter of a well-known Leiden University professor. She was to look after many people who chose to go underground. Among the many whom she cared for were my sister and brother. Though she was the bringer of mercy for many, she was eventually caught, and in the final months of the war, was taken to a concentration camp and death. We who survived all treasure her memory.

January 1943 saw me with the family Herfkens – Lenie, Piet and their son Co. As luck would have it, I was to stay with them until the war's end. This time I was not going to be kept in a room. I would be free to move in their home. I was to go out, shop and behave in a normal way. With my neutral features and blonde hair, I did not give a very different impression to the role and identity I had adopted.

Soon after my arrival at their home, the Herfkens became Aunt Lenie and Uncle Piet. This was part of an elaborate tale. I was deemed to be their niece from the Dutch East Indies, who had come over to help take care of an aunt who was suffering osteoarthritis. Never once was the truth of this story checked.

*Rosalie with the Herfkens*

I had a great zest for everything. I would go outdoors, go shopping, clean the house. My main task was to take care of Aunt Lenie. Her osteoarthritis had reached a fairly severe stage. Her hands were not able to do anything and were almost deformed. She spent most of her time in bed, though when I first came she could walk a little. Her deterioration was a tragedy to behold. Nothing helped her; whatever the doctors tried was useless.

Uncle Piet and Aunt Lenie had been school teachers. He had been the head of a Christian school. Uncle Piet was a pillar of strength in this small family. Lenie was very clever and most refined. Though thin and pale, she still emanated beauty. On many an occasion she would give me cheer when I became depressed as the war continued to drag and the worry of it overcame me. Lenie gave me some of her clothes as well as wool to knit a jumper for myself.

Everything was rationed in the war and as it dragged on, so it became scarcer. It was very hard to have food at home. However, we were lucky – Piet was in touch with one of the farmers in Leiderdorp who arranged to give us some extra milk, more or less once a week, and even on occasion some butter and eggs. Of course as 'Aunt' was ill this was a consideration, but she was a small eater so the extras were shared among us all.

Uncle Piet would also visit my parents. He knew where they were and had been taken into the confidence of the people who were caring for them. Sometimes my mother, bless her, would give him a parcel of things which she had saved despite the difficult times, and so we had something extra.

We also had a radio, a forbidden item, and indeed dangerous if caught. It was hidden in our cellar. On it we heard news from England. This station, beamed across to us Dutch, was known as Radio Oranje. Despite the dangers we listened to this bringer of good tidings and bearer of our spirits when times were at their worst.

Another amazing thing was the attitude of the neighbours. Although everyone knew me as the niece from abroad, nobody questioned me further. Perhaps, as Lenie was so ill and needed me so, my presence was taken for granted. However, the family did not question me either.

As time progressed, Aunt Lenie's suffering increased. After one arthritic attack she had to go to hospital for tests. Then I too had to travel to see her in hospital at the other end of Leiden and act as if that would have been a normal thing to do. Fortunately all went well.

Concerns for my immediate family brought sad news eventually. The actual date I cannot recall, but the nature of the news is still vivid. My parents informed me that my grandfather had died in Westerbork, that transit camp on the German border. Apparently my grandparents were at first permitted to stay put, but eventually they too were to be deported. Grandfather was already ill and died before leaving Holland. Grandmother was to be sent to Auschwitz where she perished.

My parents I was to see in the winter of 1943. It happened that Piet found out that mother was very low and suffering bouts of depression. It seemed a bit risky as I had to go by train to get there, but with my mother in such a state it was worth the risk. Needless to say it was wonderful to see them. I stayed but a few short days, but learned the nature of their lifestyle. They had to be ever so quiet when there were visitors downstairs. I believe that my father sometimes went for a short walk, but my mother never went outside from the time she went into hiding. However, my parents' safety did not last. The Germans began to use that area of Haarlem to launch their rockets at England. Everybody had to be evacuated, and fortunately my parents were found a safe abode where they remained to the end of the war.

War's end did not seem ever to come. The Germans were certainly experiencing a pounding, but somehow hung on. The last year of the war was the most difficult. We knew that Germany would lose, but the question was when. We heard of the bombed cities, of the bravery of the Russians. From our clandestine radio we heard of losses being suffered by the Germans ever since D-day. In Holland, the war dragged on. However, when liberation came, it was sweet.

On a certain day, Co Herfkens was sitting in the cellar listening to the clandestine news. Suddenly he came running out, 'Frouwke! Frouwke!' he shouted, 'come listen to the radio!' I went into the cellar and heard in French, 'Se sont rendus, se sont rendus' – 'they have surrendered'. We were all delighted, but the experience was too new, almost unreal. After two days the three Herfkens all said, 'Frouwke, it is safe to go out, the Germans are gone.' Still, I felt too fearful and dreaded going out.

The great day of freedom passed, the fear of snipers over, but still I knew nothing of my family. I was busy dusting some days later when there was a knock at the door. I looked out, and saw my parents! I could not believe it! I yelled, 'My parents are here!' and ran to the door. As I greeted them I wondered how they had found where I was living, as I had not told them.

Apparently, on one of his trips, Piet had given them my address. My parents had come from Haarlem to Leiden by boat, through the various canals – seemingly the only means of travel at the time.

My brother was brought across from his hiding place elsewhere in Leiden. I did not recognise him. Before me stood a tall fellow, pale and grown up. He had been a youngster when he was first hidden. My sister was still in Hilversum, which was not liberated for another few days.

By the twenty-third of May – my mother's birthday – we were again one united family back in Overveen. However, we were not in our former home. Our home had become occupied by another family in the meanwhile. The Dutch government had a plan by which Jewish people who had been dispossessed by the Nazis were to be given a home in return. In our case it turned out to be the house previously owned by a Dutch Nazi, now himself dispossessed and in jail.

*Rosalie (far left) with her family after the war*

Henceforth, family 'headquarters' were to be Ernst Casimirlaan 74, mother's abode for forty years until her death, aged ninety, in 1985. It was here that she welcomed her children, her grandchildren and even two great-grandchildren. Father sadly died in November 1948, surely as a result of the suffering he endured during the war.

As I travelled from Leiden to Overveen on that 23 May 1945 (on a bicycle without tyres!) I reflected on the marvel of the five of us and how we had survived the war. I thought of my brother, who had been hidden all the while at the home of a lady who had a degree in science and mathematics. At war's end he was able to sit and pass his national examinations. He subsequently became an accountant and recently retired from his last position as senior accountant of the Netherlands' prime automobile association. My sister returned to nursing, ending up as a staff nurse prior to her marriage and raising a family. I went back to the Herfkens family

*Rosalie with natural hair in 1947*

for some months until a suitable replacement carer for Lenie was found. Then I returned to the pharmacy.

Life in Holland remained difficult. Years earlier, some members of the family, including my mother's brother, had emigrated to South Africa. My sister and I felt we had nothing to lose. Within three years of the war we found ourselves there, with work permits. We remained, married, raised our families and established ourselves within the Jewish community.

My brother remained in Holland, later marrying and raising one son. My sister remains in South Africa. Some years after the death of my husband, I followed my children to Perth, Western Australia, which is where I live now, surrounded by my children, granddaughter ... and many memories.

*This narrative is an edited extract from* Five Years, *Rosalie Rothschild's self-published memoir.*

§

Rosalie and her sister moved to South Africa after the war, hoping to build a better future for themselves. An uncle of theirs was already well established there and he helped them to find work and accommodation. In South Africa Rosalie met and married Meinhold Rothschild, a German who left the country when he was sixteen to make a new life for himself in South Africa. He was a commercial traveller, and had fought in World War II in Sicily and Madagascar. They had a happy marriage, with two children, Frank and Maud.

Rosalie loved her life in South Africa and had many Dutch friends. She remained close to her sister, who also married and settled there. Rosalie worked in a Jewish aged home in Sandringham and rode her bike to work every day. When her husband passed away in 1979 and her grown-up children moved overseas, Rosalie took in boarders and became good friends with them. She was excellent with managing money, and maintained detailed accounts throughout her life.

Rosalie moved to Perth in April 1986 to be with her son, daughter, son-in-law and granddaughter. She led an active and independent life in Australia. Rosalie owned her own flat in Yokine, which she renovated herself and referred to as her 'little palace'. She drove herself around and had a busy social life, playing bridge and attending concerts with her friends.

Always generous with her time, Rosalie was one of the founding members and secretary for the ORA (Organisation of Rabbis of Australasia) and was a member of the Temple David congregation. She loved to cook and was forever making cakes, biscuits and meals for her family and friends. Her Dutch treats were

*Rosalie and Meinhold Rothschild on their wedding day*

a favourite with her children.

Although her new life in Australia separated her from her siblings and mother, she stayed in close contact and would speak to her sister for hours on the phone. Rosalie sent letters to her mother in Holland every week and travelled back to Europe to visit her. Although she loved returning to Holland, she became an Australian citizen after living in Perth for two and a half years, and was very proud of it.

Rosalie did not tell her children about her wartime experiences until they were both adults. Learning of their mother's past, Maud and Frank were amazed by her courage. At just 5'1" tall, she was described by her children as 'small but brave'. It took Rosalie many years to come to terms with her painful memories, but eventually she was able to share her story with schoolchildren through the Holocaust Institute of Western Australia. Rosalie spoke at the opening of the Anne Frank exhibition in Perth.

*Rosalie with her son Frank at a family wedding, 1985*

*Rosalie with her family at her daughter Maud's wedding, 1977*

Rosalie Rothschild passed away on 20 August 2007 and is fondly remembered by her children, granddaughter and the many people whose lives she touched.

# Rosa Levy

I was born in 1931 in the small Polish town of Rutki-Kossaki, about fifty kilometres west of Bialystok in eastern Poland. Rutki was a beautiful place, almost like a holiday resort with its forests of oak and pine trees. People would travel from Warsaw and other cities to spend their holidays there. The surrounding countryside was full of small farms. Many were dairy farms, others produced wheat and corn and other vegetables.

Our town was so small that everything was just a short walk from everything else and everybody knew each other. The Jewish community was small but there were two kosher butchers, several bootmakers, tailors and general stores. We also had a chemist and, before the war, a permanent doctor, as well as a dentist who would visit one day each month. Just outside of town were a dairy factory and a police station. Every Wednesday was market day in the town square and around the churchyard. Early in the morning, local farmers would set up small stalls displaying their produce and everyone would come along and shop for the week's supplies. There was no electricity in Rutki-Kossaki and we had to share outdoor toilets. There were two windmills owned by Jewish families.

Ours was not a large family but we were very close. My mother, whose name was Riva Warren, had three sisters – Choma, Miriam and Masha. My father's mother and brother also lived in Rutki-Kossaki. My grandparents, along with my Aunt Choma and Uncle Roovi, ran a large general store.

Our home was comfortable and happy. We lived in the rear of the house and my father, Sam Patak, ran a retail leather business in the front section. Most Jewish women in our town did not have professions but my mother was a skilled seamstress and her services were in high demand. She would visit homes all over the town to sew for people.

My mother was beloved in our village by Jewish people and non-Jews alike. She had so many friends and everywhere she went, people adored her. She was very beautiful, with fair curly hair. Everyone loved my mother; she was one of those rare people who no one had a bad word about. I thought she was an angel, and in some ways she was because I truly believe that I would not have survived the Holocaust without her.

I was the first grandchild in the family and from the time I was born I was showered with love. Every Shabbat we would gather for dinner at my grandmother's house and sometimes I would fall asleep on the couch and spend the night there. In the mornings my grandmother

*Rosa and her parents Riva and Sam Patak before the war*

would bring me hot rolls covered in halva. In 1937, when I was six years old, I started at the government school. I was one of twelve Jews in a class of forty children. I was good at my schoolwork and I got on well with all the other children.

We lived side by side with non-Jews and, while there was anti-Semitism, life was not terrible. Sometimes at school the Polish children would call out 'Jews go to Palestine'. In 1938 there was a movement to boycott Jewish stores and businesses but this failed.

In May of 1939 all the men were mobilised into the Polish army. That was the first I knew of the war. I was only a child and so it was a distant fear; I had no idea what it would mean for us. A few days after mobilisation all the men were sent home because there was no equipment and no facilities to train new soldiers.

Germany invaded Poland in September 1939 and thousands of tanks and bomber planes descended on our country as they broke through Polish defences and advanced on Warsaw. Sometime in the middle of September we heard the distant sounds of shooting in the north. Soon after that, tanks rolled into our town. My mother was five months pregnant then but she insisted that we must flee so, along with my grandmother, we ran away into the country. The front line had already advanced and bombs were being dropped from planes. It was chaos; horses were galloping away in fear through the fields and people were running for shelter, screaming in terror and searching frantically for their family members.

A farmer took us in and gave us food and a place to sleep. The next day a tank drove up to the farmhouse, which was near a main road, and an SS officer banged on the door. He took the farmer outside, ordered him to open his mouth and killed him with a single shot. We watched all of this from the window of the farmhouse. The SS officer came inside and it was a miracle that any of us survived. My father was shot in the chest and in his left hand. He lay on the floor covered in blood while we searched for sheets and towels and wet them with cold water to clean and dress his wounds.

My father was badly injured and needed medical attention so my mother found a neighbour and begged him to let us use his horse and wagon. She paid him with her wedding ring and some zlotys she had saved. While she was trying to arrange this, my mother found my Aunt Choma, who had also run away from town to escape the invasion. The two women found an old door and used it as a stretcher to carry my father onto the farmer's wagon. There was no room for us so we walked along beside the horse and cart. It took us an entire day to reach Rutki-Kossaki. Incredibly, our home was untouched. The chemist was locked up and abandoned so my mother broke a window and took some iodine and all the bandages she could find. There was no medical help anywhere for my father. Tanks were still driving through the town and everyone was in hiding.

We learned that when the Germans first arrived in the town they had killed any able-bodied males that they had been able to find. Only those who had hidden successfully or fled town had survived.

My mother was desperate to find help for my father so she walked to a German field hospital outside the town and begged the doctor to help her. The military doctor, who was German, came in an ambulance to help my father and then took him across the border to a German military hospital where he was given a blood transfusion. The Germans who helped him were under the impression that my father was simply an innocent bystander. At first they had no idea that he was a Jew. After about eight weeks he was sent to a concentration camp. We all assumed that he had died.

The Germans were still stationed in Rutki-Kossaki and we were trying as best we could to stay hidden from them. After my father was taken away my mother decided that we might be safer in Bialystok, a much bigger city where it might be easier to hide. My mother, my Aunt Choma and I set out on foot. The road was crowded with people fleeing. Sometimes we managed to get rides with people who had horses and carts but mostly we walked. It took four days to reach Bialystok. My aunt had managed to find a little bread and cheese for the journey and my mother had brought two big loaves of black bread, each weighing around ten kilograms. My mother was heavily pregnant and I begged her to let me help by carrying the bread. I threatened to stop walking and sit down on the road unless she let me help.

When we finally arrived in Bialystok we went straight to the home of a couple who were friends of my parents. Like most houses in the area, their home had been bombed and charred by fire. The husband welcomed us but he was in a dreadful state of mind because his wife had been killed the week before we arrived. He was left with their little boy and my mother helped to look after him. There was barely any food and no way to buy any. It was a terrifying time for us. I found out later that my Aunt Choma carried arsenic with her at all times in case the Germans discovered us.

We were so hungry that we decided to return to Rutki-Kossaki. When we arrived we found that our home had been taken over by another family. They refused to leave so we went to my grandmother's house and stayed with her.

Soon after this Hitler and Stalin signed a treaty and the Germans withdrew from our town and the Russian army arrived. We were so relieved by this turn of events. My father eventually returned to us. In December of 1939, my baby brother Michael was born. We called him Mischa. From the first moment I saw him I adored him.

Unfortunately it was only a temporary respite. In the summer of 1941, the Germans invaded the Soviet Union and occupied all of Poland. I was ten years old when the Germans returned to our town.

All Jews were ordered to wear yellow Stars of David on the front and back of our outer clothing so that we could be identified. Later we had to wear armbands. We were evicted from our homes and forced to live in a ghetto, which was a very small area that the Germans had designated near the school. My grandmother's home, where I had spent so many happy times, was given to a Polish family that had collaborated with the Germans. There was no fence around the ghetto and we were not guarded but Rutki-Kossaki was so small that we were easily identifiable so no one strayed outside for long. We were too terrified of being caught. Food was scarce in the ghetto and we were always hungry. Everyone had to fend for themselves. We were lucky because, before we were forced into the ghetto, my father had stored quantities of leather with Polish friends. My mother would remove her yellow star and slip out of the ghetto, retrieve some leather and barter it in the countryside for bread, butter and other food.

My Aunt Choma was expecting a baby by this time and we had nothing to use for nappies or blankets. My grandmother decided to return to her house and try and retrieve some old sheets she had stored there. She approached the Polish family and asked them if they would let her have the sheets for the baby that was coming. They refused and called the police to report her.

As she was walking home a particularly cruel German policeman we all called the Fat Sadist caught up with my grandmother near the market. A large group of Jews were working there pulling up weeds from the cobblestones. The Germans forced them to do this sort of menial labour to humiliate them. My Aunt Miriam was among them and she watched as the policeman jumped off his horse and began to beat my grandmother brutally about the face and body. He kept going until she stopped screaming and fell to the ground, covered in blood. Miriam did not know what to do so she ran home to tell my mother, begging her not to go to my grandmother for fear that she would be beaten or killed. But my mother ran to the market immediately and picked my grandmother up in her arms and carried her home. No one stopped her.

There was no medical help for Jews so my mother had to nurse my grandmother as best she could. She drifted in and out of consciousness for days and we feared that she would die. At night my mother would steal out into the fields and collect leeches to put on my grandmother's wounds. Eventually she recovered, but she was never the same. She had lost all her happiness and optimism. I never saw her smile again.

The policeman who had beaten my grandmother was a cruel and sadistic man who loved to torment the Jews. He rode through the ghetto several times a day on his white horse. He particularly loved to target a young boy called Zeitki who had a heavy limp because his left leg was much shorter than his right leg. One day I playing among some stones with three other girls and we saw the sadistic policeman approaching. Usually we ran away when we saw him but Zeitki was not able to run fast enough. The policeman drew his gun and shot a cat in the yard next to Zeitki. He called Zeitki over to where the cat was lying, gave him a knife and ordered him to cut the cat into small pieces. Zeitki was then forced to bury the cat piece by piece, running back and forth while the policeman screamed 'Faster! Faster!' at him. Finally the whole cat was buried and the policeman left. We were so relieved that Zeitki had not been killed.

My mother decided to send me away to stay with relatives in Warsaw. She knew that something was going to happen and felt that there would be no protection for Jews in the small towns. They could be liquidated so swiftly. She thought that the big cities would be safer, that there would be too many people watching for anything terrible to happen. I was sent by horse and carriage to a distant cousin in the Warsaw ghetto. She had many other relatives to care for, food was so scarce and things were very difficult. There was no time to look after a little girl.

I remember the days when the Nazis would come and pound on the doors and take people away. One day I was sent out by myself to buy a few carrots for soup. As I walked through the streets of the ghetto I saw the bodies of dead children lying in the streets. Some of them had been covered with newspapers. It was so horrifying to me to see these children simply abandoned in the gutter. There was nowhere to bury them.

I was there for about three weeks. My mother missed me terribly and felt uneasy that I was not with her so she paid a woman who was a kind of smuggler to go and bring me home. The woman did not want to be caught with me so when we were close to Rutki-Kossaki she left me in the middle of a field and pointed to some smoke coming from a house in the distance. She told me that my mother was working in that house and I should make my way to her. The snow in the fields was mounted up so high and I fell many times as I ran to find my mother. I was so happy to see her again.

One day a special SS squad arrived in town and announced that all the Jews were to be resettled in a larger city. The Polish police went from door to door ordering all Jews to pack their belongings into a single suitcase and report immediately to the market square. We were only allowed to pack twenty-five kilograms per person. I remember people running around looking for scales to weigh their belongings. My mother did not believe that we were really going to be taken to another city and so we ran to the forest to try and hide but the town was already surrounded by soldiers. Some neighbours, who we had believed were our friends, reported us to guards who were patrolling the area.

In the end we had no choice but to pack our suitcase and join the other Jews in the marketplace. Here we found most of the other members of our family. There was terrible turmoil; people were wandering through the crowd, children were crying, family members were searching for each other. People's suitcases were piled up in the street. Polish police and SS soldiers were stationed on every corner to prevent any Jews from escaping. They were being helped by ordinary Poles. One man tried to hide in the cemetery. They found him and dragged him out and beat him so badly that we could hardly recognise him.

Large tarpaulin-covered trucks began arriving in the square. I was terrified but I was with my mother. She was my strength and the wall of my survival. She pushed her way through the crowd, my baby brother in her arms, and approached the SS commander. Speaking to him in perfect German, she explained that she was a very good dressmaker and begged to be allowed to remain behind. A rumour had come out that only people with trades were going to be left behind in the ghetto. The commander told her to come back in ten minutes but when she returned he was very aggressive and said, 'What are you doing – begging for your life? Go back to where you came from.'

I decided that I was not going to be forced onto one of the trucks. Nearby, a Polish policeman was guarding an alleyway that led to the non-Jewish quarter of town.

I recognised the policeman. Before the war he had been a bootmaker and had often come to our house to buy leather from my father. Now he was helping the Germans. It was a windy day and he was struggling to light his cigarette. As he covered his face, I ran down the alley and escaped.

My mother had another sister, Masha, who had married a Pole and converted to Christianity many years before. I ran to her apartment to see if she would help me. When she opened the door to me she said, 'Oh my God, Rosa, we are all going to be killed,' but she let me in. There was laughter and the sounds of glasses clinking in the apartment below hers. People were celebrating the liquidation of the Jews. The windows of the apartment faced onto the market square where the entire Jewish community was assembled. People were being pushed, pulled and beaten to make them move faster onto the trucks. As each truck was filled, large black tarpaulins were rolled over the top and rear and secured with rope.

My aunt called out that she could see her mother – my grandmother – being pushed into the back of a truck. When she tried to lift her case into the truck a policeman hit her over the head with a club. I realised that I couldn't just save myself and leave my mother and baby brother to be taken away. I ran out of the apartment, down the steps and back through the alley to my mother and explained where I had been. My brother was sleeping in her arms. This time we all slipped past the policemen.

My aunt hid us in her storeroom. We watched through a tiny window as all our family and our friends were taken away in the trucks. We never saw anyone who was taken away that day again. We also watched as my father was separated from the others, but we had no idea where they were taking him. After the round-up, the German soldiers left. Only a few policemen remained behind.

We came out of hiding and returned to the deserted ghetto. We found out that my father had been taken away to work as slave labourer. Every day between 7 am and nightfall he worked crushing stones to repair the highway. When he worked close to our town, he was permitted to join us at night but most of the time he slept in one of several tents erected at the workplace for slave labourers.

A few weeks after the round-up, we learned from several of our old Polish neighbours that farm workers living near bushland ten kilometres from Rutki-Kossaki had been forced to dig trenches before the liquidation of the ghetto started. When the Germans left, the trenches were found to be full of bodies covered in lime. Some Poles who had hidden nearby had witnessed the executions. They said that many of the Jews had been shot. Others were thrown into the trenches and buried alive.

After the first round-up there were only a few Jews left behind. Most of them were tradespeople whose skills were needed in the town. About three months after the first deportation, a friend of my mother's came to our flat with the warning that the remaining Jews were to be rounded up and sent to a labour camp. My mother slipped out of the ghetto and set out for the countryside, hoping to find a sympathetic farmer who would agree to hide us. Two days later we received information that the round-up was to take place the next day. We hurriedly packed a few belongings. At about seven o'clock at night, we set out on the road out of the city. My father carried my brother in his arms. We removed our armbands with their yellow stars.

Two hours later we reached a farmhouse in the country. The farmer's wife knew my mother well and they were very sympathetic. They gave us food and let us sleep in their barn. At about 4 am we were woken and told that the Germans were surrounding the area and that we must run away as quickly as possible. We had to decide what to do with my brother. It would be impossible to run fast or to hide with a small child. The farmer and his wife had three children of their own and they agreed to look after my brother. They would pretend that he was their child.

We left the farm and ran into the nearby forest. We were not the only ones hiding from the Germans in those woods. There were screams coming from every direction as the soldiers shot at people. I heard bullets whistling past. One came so close to me that I thought it was a bird grazing my shoulder. We ran deeper into the forest. In the end, I dropped to the ground exhausted and managed to crawl under a large bush. The soldiers ran right past me, less than a metre away.

I had lost my father in the chaos. It seemed like a miracle when we suddenly came face to face. As we walked on, we came across a young man who was also on the run from the Germans. He said that it was too risky to be with a child and went off by himself. Later that day we learned from a farmer's wife that he had been caught by ordinary Poles and handed over to the SS. The Nazis were offering a reward of one kilo of sugar and one litre of kerosene for every Jew captured and delivered. That was the price of a Jewish life.

We walked in the direction we had seen my mother take. My father knew the area well and we walked all night, using back roads that were very swampy. We had no food and by the following afternoon we were cold, hungry and exhausted. Suddenly a man came running after us, whistled out and called my name. We couldn't believe it. When he caught up to us, he told us that my mother was hiding in his farmhouse and had seen us. So the three of us were finally reunited. The farmer's wife and my mother were very good friends, but it was too risky for us to stay. Anyone found hiding Jews would be killed. We left soon after.

For several months we lived on the run, moving from place to place. For a few weeks we hid in a cornfield, crouching between the high stalks of corn. There was a sympathetic farmer nearby and sometimes he would bring us a bit of soup. We had a little blanket with us. I don't know how on earth we came by it but it was the only thing we had to keep us warm at night. Sometimes it would rain and we would hold the blanket wrapped around us, wringing it out when the rain stopped. When the autumn came we knew we had to leave. It was growing colder and soon the corn would not be high enough to hide in.

In December 1942, we were taken in by a kind and very religious Catholic Polish farmer. His name was Godleswski. He hid us in a hayloft in his barn. Only he and his daughter, whose name was Frania Sleszynki, knew we were there. No one else in the farmer's household, including his wife, his mother-in-law or his farmhands, knew that we were hidden there. It was so dangerous for them to shelter us.

The hayloft was located above a pig sty. It was tiny, perhaps two metres long by one metre wide and very dusty, but it became our home for nearly two years. The farmer's main crop was peas and there was a large supply stored in the loft, which became our staple diet. Sometimes the farmer's daughter would bring some bread, coughing three times to tell us that she had food for us. We would divide the bread into three portions but my mother would keep some of hers aside. When I woke up in the night crying with hunger, she would give me her bread. She was so hungry that she would often faint. I would pat her face and beg her to wake up.

We were always hungry. Worse still was our constant thirst. My father would sometimes sneak out at night to get water from the farmyard. This was extremely dangerous as the farmer's dog wouldn't stop barking. Other times we collected drops of rainwater in a cup and drank it. We were lucky to drink half a cup of water a week. We couldn't wash. When it rained we would splash our faces clean. In the wintertime it was freezing. We would remove a floorboard and use the pig sty as a toilet.

We couldn't move around or exercise and we couldn't make any noise at all. The days were so long, hidden there in that tiny space. The farmer's daughter brought me some Christian religious books and I would read them again and again. My father found a little board and made a kind of Monopoly game. He made figures out of tiny pieces of bread and we played to try and make the time pass. At one time my mother feared that she was pregnant. It would have been a disaster for us. How could she have given birth in that place, or kept a baby quiet so we would not be found? Luckily for us, she was not pregnant.

Once the Germans came and searched the farm. We were sure that we would be killed. They threw down several bales of hay but the barn became so dusty that they left, not believing that anyone could be hidden in such a place.

We did not know it at the time but the farmer was also sheltering another Jew. One of his housemaids was a Jewish woman who was pretending to be Polish. We only found out afterwards. Everywhere people were trying to disguise themselves, to hide who they were to save their lives.

We stayed hidden in the hayloft for twenty-two months, until the Russians returned in October 1944. When we were finally freed, our legs were so bent and stiff from crouching in the loft for all that time that we could hardly walk. We tried to make our way home to Rutki-Kossaki but we could only manage a few steps before we had to sit down on the road and rest.

There was no one from our family left. Most of the Jews of our town were gone. We searched for my little brother, who had been only three years old when we left him in the care of a Polish farmer. Eventually we found out that after my mother, father and I had left, my brother had cried continually, searching for us and calling out my name. The farmer let him out for a little while to show him that we were not there but he was distraught and many people heard him crying. The next morning the Nazis visited the farm and questioned the farmer about his family. Neighbours had informed them that the crying child did not belong to the farmer. He pretended that my brother had been left in his care by pedlars but the Germans took him away to their local headquarters. Apparently they took a liking to him and would take him out for walks. He was eventually identified as a Jew and deported to Auschwitz.

A survivor of Auschwitz saw my brother, my grandmother and my Aunt Choma's little girl. My grandmother looked after both children. My father's friend Itzruk Borshten saw them just for a little while. The only one in my family to survive apart from my mother, father and me was my mother's sister Miriam, who had escaped to Russia.

Those weeks after the war ended were so strange. Those who had survived were coming out of the camps and out of hiding, walking skeletons. They were searching for their families, for anyone they knew. I remember that time so clearly. People had survived, they were happy. They danced in the street. But they were also haunted. So many of them couldn't bear life anymore. I remember one woman who had been forced to kill her baby. They had been in hiding and the baby wouldn't stop crying so they made her suffocate it. How could she live with what she had been forced to do? She killed herself when the war was over.

My mother was incredible. We had nothing but she wanted the people coming out of the concentration camps to have somewhere to come and eat so she opened a little restaurant. She searched in the ruined homes for whatever she could find – a broken oven, a few plates, a cloth. She cooked the most incredible things out of almost nothing on an oven that barely worked.

The people coming out of Auschwitz and the other camps had no homes to go to. My mother found mattresses and set them up all over our house so people could sleep there. There was nowhere else for them to go.

The end of the war wasn't the end of the hatred of the Jews. In March 1945, hostile Poles shot and killed my mother. She was only thirty-two years old. My father was also wounded but he survived and was taken to hospital. My mother lay in the streets for days, while policemen watched over her body to make sure no one took it away. I was so distressed that I approached the policeman and asked him to kill me too because I had nothing to live for. He told me to come back that night when nobody was around and he would kill me.

Non-Jewish neighbours let me stay with them. It was the worst time of my life. I cried so much. I remember one of the nights in the Polish family's house, their little girl called out to her mother for a drink of water. 'Where is my mother?' I remember thinking. She could never come to me again. I was thirteen years old.

After my mother was killed, my father and I left Poland and went to a displaced persons camp in Germany. We weren't supposed to leave Poland but we couldn't stay there after what had happened. We spent three years in that camp. There were many educated people there, doctors and scholars and teachers, and they decided that those few children who had survived should go back to school again. They managed to open a small school in Munich and I was able to attend. I had to start from the very beginning and everything was in Hebrew, which made it even harder for me.

I had a very good friend called Chaya. We decided that we must have everything that we had lost. One of the things we dreamed of was learning to play the

*Rosa (centre) with friends in the DP camp after the war*

piano so we traded our bread rations for piano lessons. Our teacher told us that Chaya was not good enough to be a serious pianist but that I was talented and that I must continue. In the end Chaya emigrated to Israel and went to a music conservatorium there and became a piano teacher. I had to give up music. Life was hard in the early days in Australia and there was no time for such things. I had to study, to learn a trade, to work and then to raise my family.

In 1948, when I was seventeen years old, we migrated to Australia. My mother's sister had come back from Russia by then and my father married her so that we could all go to Australia together. No one wanted to stay in Europe after what had happened.

Those first days were so difficult. We had no money and spoke no English. Some cousins in North Perth took us in and let us stay in one of their bedrooms. My father found a job washing bottles in a milk factory, but he later became a successful wool buyer.

I went to City Commercial College to learn to read and write English, as well as other skills such as shorthand and typing. The fees were thirty pounds per year and I had to work to pay them off.

When I was eighteen, my aunt gave birth to a little boy, Max. I thought that God had given me another brother. Of course it was not the same, he could not replace the brother I had lost, but I loved him so much. I would take him on walks to Hyde Park. Once he fell in the water because he was trying to catch a duck. He adored me.

I became a milliner and spent time working in Melbourne and Sydney. You could earn much more there than in Perth. I missed my family though and when I heard that my little brother had burned his hands badly by touching the radiator, I decided to move back to Perth.

Not too long after I returned to Perth, I married Julian Miller. I had known him for some time. He worked as a wool buyer like my father. Soon we had two little boys, Allan and Robin. We both loved them madly. They were such good boys.

Julian had been in Auschwitz during the war. He had been sent there with his mother and they were separated into different barracks but they made a pact that they would catch sight of each other every day through the wires. Every day they would make sure that the other one was still alive. They did this for so long, always searching for each other. Then one day his mother was gone. He never saw her again.

Julian and I didn't want to tell our children about the things that had happened to us in the war so we never

*Rosa on her wedding day with her younger brother Max*

spoke about it in front of them. At night though, when they were sleeping, we would make ourselves cups of coffee and sit and talk. He would talk about his family and I would talk about mine.

We bought a block of land in Coolbinia and began to build a house. It was such an exciting thing to do – creating our own home. Every day I would go and check on progress. I love gardening and I had the most beautiful garden at that house.

We also opened a little delicatessen in the Menora supermarket, selling all sort of European and Jewish foods that weren't available in other shops. There was no cream cheese back then so I would sour the milk and make my own.

When the boys were still young, Julian became ill with kidney failure. He was on dialysis for three years and he died when he was only forty-five years old. I had to support my children so I worked very hard. I was a

*Rosa's father Sam and her sons Robin and Allan in Perth*

good cook so I had a little catering business and I also studied childcare so that I had something else I could do to make a little money. Eventually I was able to buy some investment properties and things became a little easier.

I eventually married again, to an American I had met while visiting cousins in New York. However, the marriage did not work out. My third husband was Don Levy, who I had known for many years here in Perth. Sadly he died after falling down on the street and striking his head on the pavement.

I have five grandchildren and one great-grandchild and I have been blessed with many wonderful friends here in Perth. I play bridge and canasta and sometimes just sit in the garden in the sun.

I went back to Poland only once, much later in my life. I went to the house in Rutki-Kossaki where I had

*Rosa in Poland, outside the house where she was born*

been born but a man stared at me from the window as if I should not be there and I could not ask to go inside. There is nothing left in Poland for me. For many years I sent gifts and money to the Polish farmer who saved our lives. Every year at Christmas time I would send them a big parcel.

When the Holocaust Institute was started in Perth, they asked me to come and tell my story to the students. It is not easy to speak about these things but I do it because it is important that the children know and that what happened to the Jews is remembered. I've received so many beautiful letters from the children and their teachers thanking me for speaking to them.

For sixty-five years after the war I did not dream about my mother. I dreamed about everything and everybody else but never my mother. Then, not so long ago, when I was going through a terrible time in my life, I was lying in bed crying and my mother's face appeared.

*Rosa with her family in Perth*

My mother's beautiful face, just as I remembered her. It was as if she had come to comfort me. She was my strength, the reason for my survival. Without her, I would not have lived through the war. I would not be here today to tell my story.

## *Aaron Landau*

I was born on the twenty-ninth of May in 1915 in a small town in central Poland called Radomsko. The population of Radomsko was around twenty thousand people and approximately one thousand of these were Jewish. The town was surrounded by little villages and the closest big city was Lodz.

I was the youngest in a family of eight children – seven boys and one girl. My only sister Fela was the second youngest. When I was born two of my oldest brothers were already married and one had a child, so I had a nephew who was older than I was. When I was only six months old my mother died of typhoid fever. My father married a widow with four children of her own. Two of them came to live with us and our home became very crowded. I remember that the children slept three to a bed.

We were a poor family. My father was a very religious man who earned his living as a teacher of Hebrew and religious studies. Students came to our home for lessons. My father was my first teacher, but he soon found that it was difficult to teach his own son and sent me to a friend of his for lessons in Jewish studies. When I was eight years old I was enrolled in the local Jewish school and there I learned the Polish language and history, geography and mathematics.

We lived in a Jewish area of town, but still experienced anti-Semitism. As a religious Jew, I wore a yarmulke or head covering when in the street and I can remember being called names by Polish children. From my earliest years, I felt insecure when I was outside my own home.

The period following the First World War was a time of poverty in Poland. Two of my older brothers moved to the nearby city of Lodz in search of work. We had barely enough to eat and my brother suggested to my father that we should all move to Lodz where they could help to support the family. So in 1927, when I was twelve years old, we moved to Lodz and lived with my older brothers in a rented flat in the city.

I was apprenticed to a tailor for three and a half years. I earned no money at all; my brothers had to pay him to teach me the trade. When I was sixteen years old I finally began to earn some money. I can still remember how good it felt to have my first wages in my pocket.

We had heard of the persecution of the Jews in Germany and my stepmother's uncle, who had looked after two of her children from the time she had married my father, had sold up his business and moved to Palestine.

War broke out in September 1939 and Germany immediately invaded Poland. Lodz was in the west of a country in which the borders had changed many times. I was afraid of the Germans and decided to run away to Warsaw, which was well over a hundred kilometres east of Lodz. I thought that going east would be safer.

I went on foot, carrying what I could with me. The journey took three days and for some of the way I got lifts from people who had horses and carts. Food was scarce. The war had thrown the country into chaos. I was very hungry and lined up in a queue for bread with other Poles in Warsaw. A Polish man pointed me out as a Jew and I was taken out of the queue and beaten up. I can still remember this. I did not feel safe in Warsaw. There were people fleeing further east to the city of Bialystok, close to the border of Russia. This also involved a long journey on foot. I joined the people travelling east and was very lucky to find work in Bialystok. The tailor I worked for gave me a bed in his home.

Shortly afterwards, as arranged between Hitler and Stalin, the Russians took over the eastern part of Poland and arrived in Bialystok. At first food was plentiful and I was able to send food parcels to my father, who was still in Lodz. My two older brothers in Lodz decided to follow me and escape to Bialystok. I later found out from survivors that they had both been shot and killed while trying to cross the border out of the German-occupied part of Poland.

In 1940 the ghettoes were established in Lodz and my father and stepmother, along with two of her children and an uncle and aunt, were forced to leave their flat and move into one room in the ghetto. I lost touch with them.

I remained free in Bialystok until the Germans invaded Russia and took over the eastern part of the country. It was time to escape again. This time I fled into the nearby forest with a group of about thirty other Jews. This particular forest was very thickly wooded and stretched for many kilometres in all directions. It was summertime.

I remember that the first person I saw when I entered the forest was a Jewish man and he was praying. I greeted him in Hebrew and he told me that his two sons were also in hiding with him. We became friends.

When we went into the woods we took what we could carry with us and dug bunkers in the ground to sleep in, covering ourselves with branches of trees at night. We stole potatoes and other vegetables from the surrounding fields and some people who had money or valuables exchanged these for food. This was a dangerous practice because the Poles would often give up Jews to the Germans. For each Jew handed over, a Pole would receive a litre of kerosene and a kilo of sugar.

Russian and Polish soldiers were also hiding from the Germans in the woods and Partisan groups were organised. Our group of thirty Jews joined the Partisans. At first we had no weapons to defend ourselves with, but the Russians and Poles had guns.

I lived in the woods with the Partisans for three years until the liberation. Less than half of our group survived. We only attacked German soldiers when they were travelling along the roads at night. Sometimes we walked backwards when we left the forest to leave false tracks for the Germans in case they tried to follow us. We blew up their vehicles and had gun battles with them. We took guns from the dead German soldiers, as well as whatever else we needed to survive such as clothing and food.

We left the forest quickly and, when our mission was completed, went straight back into the depths of the woods. The Russians shared their food with us and we fought side by side. We felt much safer with the Russians than we did with the Poles.

When the winter came it was terrible in the forest. It was bitterly cold – many degrees below zero. We killed sheep, eating the meat and using the skins to try to keep warm. Fortunately there was plenty of wood and we lit fires for warmth. In looking back, I really don't know how I survived.

In the summer of 1944, the Russian army counterattacked the Germans and began moving towards Germany. Where we were hiding was not far from Bialystok and when we heard the shooting and saw the German army retreating, we returned to the city. The Russians were there, helping themselves to food and clothing and sending parcels home to Russia, where these things were in short supply.

In a few weeks the Russians organised an army of Poles under their command. I volunteered to join. I would have been conscripted anyway and I felt very strongly that I wanted to fight the Germans who had destroyed my family.

One day I saw an officer with torn trousers and offered to mend them. He said, 'So we have a tailor here!' From then my job was to be a tailor for the army. I had to sew up their parcels. Later they obtained material and I had to make clothing and uniforms and do their mending as well. They even sent clothes I had made home to their families.

I moved with the army towards Berlin, on a truck with a sewing machine and flat irons, which were what we used to press fabric and had to be heated on a fire. We stopped at many towns and villages along the way and whenever we halted I got out my sewing machine and got to work. When we came close to Berlin an officer said to me, 'Enough of tailoring. We need every soldier to help us take Berlin.'

There was fighting on the streets and the Germans retreated, mostly without resistance. When we approached the Reichstag, where the German parliament was, we saw that it was burning. I am not very tall so I asked someone to let me stand on their shoulders. Then, as an act of defiance, I wrote my name in Yiddish on the wall of the Reichstag.

In 1945 I had leave from the Russian army and I went back to Lodz to look for my family. The ghetto there had been totally destroyed and of course it was empty. All I found were a few family photographs. I never knew exactly what happened to my family. No one was alive to tell me. My father, my stepmother, my stepsisters, my brothers and their families, my uncles, aunts and cousins – all of them had perished.

Then a wonderful thing happened. I found my sister Fela. She had escaped to Russia during the war and had also come back to search for our family. Fela had the address of an uncle who had gone to live in England. Although his house had been bombed, he was alive and living in London. He was to play an important part a little later in my life.

While I had been travelling on the road to Berlin with the army, we had come across two Jewish girls by the roadside. They had come from an abandoned concentration camp. I asked my commanding officer if they could come with us to help me with my tailoring. One of the girls appealed to me very much. Her name was Sarah.

When I returned to Berlin from Lodz after my leave was up, I met up with Sarah again and we decided that I would desert the army and we would escape to the American zone of East Berlin. This was relatively easy to do. I left my army uniform in a toilet in East Berlin and changed into other clothes and we moved across the border.

In East Berlin I met someone who looked Jewish and discovered that there was a Jewish camp run by the Joint Distribution Committee, which was a special agency run by American Jews for the relief of Jews in Europe. We could have gone to the camp but Sarah and I did not want to stay in the country that had destroyed our lives. We had no identification papers but we managed to buy some illegally, so we were able to travel by train to France.

In Paris I found a cousin and her three children. She had lived in Paris from before the war and was among the only survivors of our large family. We stayed in the city for a few days with a group of Jewish refugees. One day a Hungarian man came looking for a tailor. He offered me a job and a place for us to sleep. He also arranged papers for Sarah and me to remain legally in Paris. Later my cousin found a room for us in the house where she lived. We stayed with her until my uncle who had been living in London came to Paris to meet us. This was in 1949.

In the meantime, Sarah and I were married and our daughter Danielle was born in 1950. When she was only a few months old, my uncle invited us to come and live with him in London. We lived with him in his home and he gave me work as a tailor.

Danielle married and migrated to Australia and in 1979 I came to Perth to visit her. She arranged for me to remain here and I have lived in Australia ever since. I started a small factory and manufactured school uniforms. I feel that Australia is my home.

*Not much is known about Aaron's life in Australia and the whereabouts of his descendants.*

# Erica Moen

I was born in Loosdrecht in Holland in 1924. My parents, Levie and Marianna Deen, grew up in Amsterdam, where they continued to live when they were first married. There was a large Jewish community in Amsterdam and generally the Jewish people were poor. My parents decided, when they began to raise a family, that they wanted their children to do better than themselves. With two other friends they purchased large blocks of land in Loosdrecht and built houses. My father had established a factory for making furniture and a house made from timber was transported from Amsterdam's harbour to Loosdrecht. That's where I grew up with my parents, three sisters and two brothers.

My father was an architect and interior designer.

*The house in Loosdrecht*

He also designed furniture and lighting. The name Deen is familiar to many Dutch people today who have an interest in furniture. Even now his furniture is being advertised as being made by L. Deen. Father was continually looking for a speciality design for his furniture such as making a chair out of one piece of material. Unfortunately, he was not a businessman but an idealist. Consequently he was severely affected financially in the Depression of the 1930s.

My father was a good man, one of the best. He would share my mother's cakes with his neighbours. He wore only pure cotton garments and no leather shoes. He was a vegetarian and loved to walk barefoot, in touch with nature. He was a great walker – he would have walked around the world given the opportunity.

My mother started a self-help women's group during the Depression when food was very scarce. My parents were socialists, in what was becoming a strong movement in those years, and did all they could

*Levie Deen (far left) with guests in Nieuw Loosdrecht, 1920*

to promote socialist ideas trying to obtain better living conditions for the poor.

In our home there was enough food. I had one dress and one pair of shoes and I was never cold. We all helped with the housework. Mother worked as a secretary in the business. We usually had a girl who lived in, like an au pair, many of whom were from Austria.

I suppose we were more socialistic than Jewish, and were not very observant. My grandmother used to bring us matza on Pesach in a large box that looked like a hatbox. Both my parents had come from Orthodox Jewish families. Father remembered how his mother always washed the doorstep ready for Shabbat. However, many had left the Jewish way. We were not taught Hebrew and there was no shule where we lived in Loosdrecht.

My father's and mother's families had been in Holland for at least two hundred and fifty years. The first

*Wooden pots made by Levie Deen*

known record of our ancestors was that of Abraham Wolf Deen, born in Amsterdam in approximately 1739. He was a street-seller by occupation and married Anna Joseph Gans. We spoke Dutch at home although we knew and spoke a few Yiddish words. There were many Jews in Amsterdam who spoke Dutch mixed with Yiddish and to this very day the Dutch language contains many Hebrew words. Holland was noted for its non-persecution of Jews and that's why, when the Germans invaded, it was so hard to accept that we were not free anymore and why so many were killed. The Jewish population before the war was 140,000. Around 107,000 were deported. Seventy-five per cent of the Dutch Jewish population was murdered. Compared with other western countries this was very high.

Loosdrecht was about thirty kilometres from Amsterdam. There were three Jewish families in town with whom we mixed, none of them religious. The children of one of those families now live in Israel.

*Levie and Marianna Deen and their young family, c. 1930*

The first school I went to was in Hilversum. It was a primary school and privately owned by the headmaster. It received a government subsidy and operated under a quota system. At the government schools only the three 'R's were taught, so I was privileged to attend the Hilversum school where handicrafts, weaving, cricket and hockey were taught. The school was co-educational. After primary school I went on to high school, where I stayed for three years. I wanted to become a physical education teacher.

Even though we lived in a country where there was no discrimination, I always felt it. Do everything right and you could still be called a dirty Jew. On a visit by a neighbour the young daughter called me a dirty Jew. Her mother apologised, saying, 'She did not learn that from us,' so I was always aware of it. I believed it was taught by the churches. Yet I still had a large circle of non-Jewish friends – very nice people: teachers,

*Deen family in Loosdrecht, c. 1930*

lawyers, doctors – who undoubtedly contributed to my survival.

I was sixteen when the war broke out. We couldn't believe what had been happening in Germany. We had looked after some Jewish people from Poland who told us, but we couldn't believe it. We certainly didn't believe anything like that could happen in Holland. We had a group of Jewish children who had fled from Austria and Germany, some of whom stayed at our home in Loosdrecht. They lived with different farmers to learn how to milk cows and work the land. They were training for living in Palestine but they never did get there. Most of these children were killed in Holland by the Germans.

In 1940 the Germans came. We had to carry an identity card stamped with the letter 'J'. The Jews were required to give themselves up and to assemble at certain places. Why those Jews gave themselves up

*Deen family before the war*

remains a mystery to me. I suppose they did so because they didn't think anything would be done to them. I know one family that didn't register and most of that family survived. I was only sixteen, still at school and busy there. I was not afraid and that's the worst part. We should have been. The Nazis came to the school and threw me out and that was it.

I went to a Jewish school for a while with Jewish teachers, but it got too dangerous and I left. I then went to learn woodwork and sculpture with a woodworker but it also became too difficult. We were not allowed to travel. We were not allowed to go to school or to contact other people. We were not allowed to do anything. I didn't know what was taking place. I just stayed at home and taught my younger brother and sister. My parents didn't speak about what was happening; they couldn't see evil in anyone or anything. All my father said was, 'It doesn't matter, we will be all right, we haven't done anything wrong.' They rented a pensione called the

*Hotel Nieuwe Brug in 1949*

Nieuwe Brug Restaurant and Mother attended to the business part. My oldest son, Martin, was born there after the war. Anybody could come as our family was well liked and that's how we managed to live.

In 1942 papers arrived with instructions for me, my two sisters and my brother to report to the camp of Westerbork. At the time it was considered that my parents were too old and the younger children too young to work for the Germans. Jews from many other villages were transported to Amsterdam. Right from the beginning the Jewish people were being grouped together. My boyfriend came from a very orthodox family living in Hilversum. The Nazis came and took away his parents and brothers. He crawled under the sofa when he saw them coming and so escaped. He came to our house straight away. He told me what happened and said I should not go to Westerbork but pack my bag and go away with him, which I did. I packed my toothbrush and left. I never said goodbye. I just left. I've no idea what made me do it. I'd never stayed away from my parents before.

He took me to Hilversum to the home of two elderly non-Jewish people where we stayed the night. In the morning the old people had hysterics. They were so frightened and told us we would have to go.

We moved again to non-Jewish friends – the father was a teacher of handicapped children. They were wonderful people and I stayed there until one day the baker saw me through the window and after that it became too dangerous. I knew I had been discovered and our hosts contacted the Dutch underground. Someone, not Jewish, arranged transport for me to the east of Holland. If I had been of fair complexion it would have been easier to hide, but having dark hair and features, I could more easily be recognised as Jewish.

At that time I received the new identity of Henny van der Linden. Although a new card was provided by the underground and the old one destroyed, I was always on the run and afraid to use it.

I was sent to a minister of religion on the other side of Holland. My boyfriend now found his own way. I was then sent to a farm in Lemelerveld where I was hidden. The people, Hendrik and Mina Grootemarsink, were very good to me. If anyone came I could hide in the ceiling, and if there was not enough time, behind a door. I couldn't go outside in case I was seen. I didn't feel I was badly done by because I could be in the house and hide when someone came. I didn't feel cross or angry by this turn of events, but a time came when I didn't feel safe. I had no hiding place.

One day, near the farm, a group of twelve Jewish people who had been hiding in a small hut were

*The Grootemarsink farmhouse, 1945*

betrayed. For at least a week before that I had been feeling very unsafe and so I made a little cubby, built of two bales of hay and a cover, behind the cowshed. On the Sunday I saw a big truck with a white cover approaching the farmhouse. I was frightened and fled into the cubby. The men who came were Dutch Nazis and they shot bullets through the hay trying to find me. Everyone was very frightened.

Two weeks later they found another Jewish girl who had been hiding with me. They picked her up on the roadside as she was riding her bike and she never came back. But they couldn't find me. It was a miracle. The Nazis took the farmer and told his wife that I was to report to the Nazis the next day at six o'clock in the morning to set the farmer free. Minister Kerrs came and said to me: 'Don't go.' Like a miracle the farmer was released and came back the following afternoon. The Nazis came back several times to see if I was there but I stayed hidden in the wheat field.

I was then sent to another farm but now had lost all control and suffered from what can be called amnesia. I had no idea where I was and I was very frightened and anxious. If I saw a white cow I thought it was a white truck. I became hysterical and had to be moved through the Dutch underground to the city of Apeldoorn. I was in the home of an old minister of religion, the brother of the one who had first helped me. From his place I went to various homes where I could help with the young children and the cooking. I was hiding all the time and couldn't show my face. The Nazis came one time and I was hidden under the floor of the church. There were rats there and they wanted to eat the food that I had been given. It was not only dangerous for me but also for those who looked after me. Eventually I was brought out. I had only been there for two days but it felt like two years. The Nazis were always hunting for hidden Jews and also for the things belonging to the Jews, like paintings and jewellery and other valuable items.

I was moved from there, from one place to the next, for three and a half years. I can't recall all the places but I know the people who arranged it were two brothers and their sister in the underground. They kept me hidden from the Nazis all those years. I had no contact with any of my family and I had no idea what had happened to them or where they were. I was always frightened by other people and hid all the time. Many times I just managed to escape the Nazis.

In May 1945 the Canadian armed forces came through on tanks and freed us. I sat on top of a tank and felt so happy. To get home and find my family I needed to cross the Ijssel River. I was now twenty-one. I had packed a bag and was taken to the river. I was prepared to swim over to the other side when a Canadian soldier stopped me and said he would help. But instead of taking me across the river he took me into a bush. I hadn't mixed with boys and I was extremely frightened. I begged him to let me go, which he did. I eventually went to the home of Jan and Dinnie van Zutphen. Jan was a well-known person who had started a charitable trust many years previously funded from the sale of diamond scrapings and built a hospital for tuberculosis patients.

It was there I found my mother. She had been with him throughout the entire war. It was not a happy reunion. Although she found sanctuary there, she had been overworked and was in a very upset frame of mind. She just cried the whole time. Then my youngest brother Lou, who had been hidden by friends in the underground, arrived. He was stooped

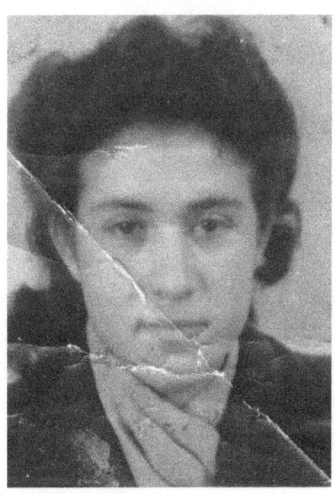

*Erica Deen, December 1945*

from the cramped conditions and the sight in his right eye had deteriorated. He eventually studied medicine and became a professor of anaesthesia. Eventually my father also came back.

Trouble started after the war. Father had been hidden in the home of two elderly schoolteachers who had become very fond of him. When he came back he brought these two elderly ladies with him. It was too hard for him to just leave these people after all they had done for him. My sister Sonja had been hidden on a farm. She was later honoured for bravery by the Dutch, American and English governments. Towards the end of the war American and British servicemen parachuted onto the farm property and she used to rescue them as well as send out radio messages to the allies. One of these American servicemen was later shot in front of her by the Nazis in a drunken stupor. Sonja would also have been shot but she admitted that she was Jewish and was spared and sent to Westerbork. She was later freed by the Dutch underground.

My youngest sister Ellen was hidden in an attic with twelve other children. They were betrayed and sent to Westerbork. They were all transported to the Hague where they were imprisoned for some time. She was a gorgeous girl, only nine or ten years of age at the time. One of the female guards of Westerbork took her home. She was not Jewish but married to a Jewish man. They were French and took her to France where she was sent to a boarding school. She was the only one who, through the Red Cross, knew I was alive after the war. Eventually she married a very orthodox Jew and went to live in Amsterdam. Two of her three children now live in Israel. She died there of cancer in 1987.

My brother Lou was hidden and went from attic to cellar time and time again. He was only seven or eight years old and thought he was being teased. He thought he was being kept in jail by the people who cared for him, so he wouldn't go back to see them ever again after the war. He didn't speak about it, but his grievance was such that he couldn't go back. This he told me when I went back to Holland for a holiday later.

This certificate is awarded to

Sonja Deen

as a token of gratitude for and appreciation of the help given to the Sailors, Soldiers and Airmen of the British Commonwealth of Nations, which enabled them to escape from, or evade capture by the enemy.

1939-1945

Air Chief Marshal,
Deputy Supreme Commander,
Allied Expeditionary Force

*Sonja Deen's certificate of appreciation, 1945*

The family, as it came together, began to look for a home. We asked the mayor of Loosdrecht for a place. We leased a home until we could go back to our own. We had no money. I managed to work for a couple of weeks in an office, and then I started nursing for a while. I went back to help my parents build their lives again. The Jewish community gave us two thousand guilders, which we were to pay back without interest. It was spent very quickly and mother had the worry of paying it back.

My older brother Harold and sister Rebecca didn't come back. They had been hidden on a farm. The farmer's labourer had a fight with the farmer and gave him away to the Nazis who came and took them away. They both died in Sobibor on 16 July 1943.

I've never spoken about it before. People don't know about Holland but all conversations come back to it. We were always told not to talk about the war because no one wanted to hear. Dutch Jews who went to settle in other countries like South Africa immediately after the war warned visiting relatives not to mention their war experiences. I know several instances of this. My parents never mentioned their son and daughter who perished. They never talked about it. They never discussed what happened.

After those three or four years of what happened to us under the Nazi occupation it was a fight to start life again. My mother lost her mother, two brothers and a sister, nephews and nieces. Father came from a family of nine of whom one was safe in England and two in Holland survived. The rest perished, all gone. My father never said a word. Now my eldest son Martin wants to talk about it and bring it back.

*Harold Deen, 1940*

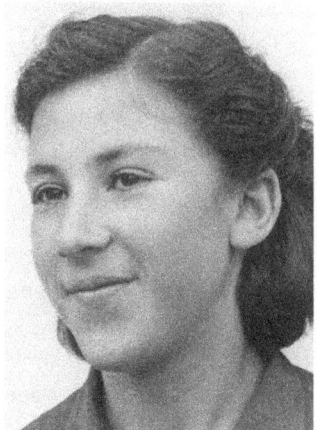
*Rebecca Deen, 1940*

That is good but it is unpleasant for me because it makes me remember. People talk about six million who died. I can't comprehend the death of six million people.

Soon after the war ended I took up some semblance of normal life. I'd had three Jewish boyfriends but I didn't want to marry any of them. Then I met my future husband, Klaas, and fell in love at once. He had joined the Dutch underground army at the age of eighteen after he had been called up to go to Germany to work as slave labour in 1943. From that day he hid in the fields until he joined the underground. He took part in sabotage activities, blowing up bridges, handling weaponry and helping people who were in hiding. All the time these underground fighters were exposed to great danger from the Germans. We had been married for one year when our son Martin was born.

My husband was keen to emigrate and in 1949 he applied for a permit to South Africa. The permit contained a reference to 'no Jews' and had been scored out. That was enough to put us off. A friend of my husband's had been in Brisbane while serving in the navy during the war. He was a pastry cook and a chocolatier. He said, 'What about going to Australia? There's room for us in Brisbane.'

We were still living at home with my parents. It was not good in Holland; everything was topsy-turvy after the war. My husband said to me, 'If you want to go, we go.' We applied, were accepted and ready to go within three weeks. Our friend, as it happened, was rejected. So my husband went to Australia and I was to follow twelve months later. We had no language, no money and we came to Perth because the fare was cheaper than to Brisbane.

I came with our son Martin on the SS *Volendam*, a migrant ship. There was a beautiful dining room which we went to on the first day. The seas were very rough and I had to tie Martin to the chair. I never saw the dining room again, I was so seasick.

My husband had written to me that everything was good here. But it wasn't at first. I think if my parents had known how difficult it was going to be they would have done everything to stop me. My husband had looked for a house for us. He couldn't even find part of a house. He saw an advertisement in the paper for a property in Bedfordale. It only had a shed and a weatherboard house on it, but the deposit was a mere ten pounds, so he bought it.

When we arrived at Fremantle, it was terribly hot. We had to schlepp the cases and the playpen over the bridge to get the train to Perth. From there we caught the train to Armadale. Then we got a taxi to take us to our place. The taxi got a flat tyre and as we were near a pub we all went in there to wait for repairs. It was dark when we eventually arrived at our new home.

I was young and happy and ready to accept everything. The house was like a castle to us. There was no electricity, no toilet, nothing. But we were free! I still have it in my bones. I want to be free. I'm lucky I'm free. I can do what I like. People don't realise what it's like to be free.

We developed an orchard. We cleared the land and put in fruit trees. We grew apples, pears, kiwi fruit, mandarins and oranges and from these we made a living. We also grew vegetables and sold some of the produce by the roadside. In recent years we retired, sold off two-thirds of the property and built a new home on the remaining land.

My parents actually migrated to Australia after the 1956 Russian invasion of Hungary. They were frightened at the possibilities of war in Europe and came to live with us in Perth. They were happy here. But at their age they missed their friends and way of life and returned to Holland, although they did revisit us from time to time. Their last visit was in 1977 when my mother came to see our granddaughter, Rebecca, who was named after my sister who died in the camps. My grandmother's name was also Rebecca.

When I first came here I didn't want to be Jewish at all. I didn't want my children ever to go through the same experience, but you can't really stop being Jewish because people won't let you. In the early days I was helping a neighbour who had a disabled child. I got on well with her and liked her very much. One day in conversation she mentioned the words 'the dirty Jews'. I was upset with this remark and another neighbour whom I met going home took me in and explained that Christ was a Jew. I could not believe it. So even here you can't get away from anti-Semitic attitudes. Now it doesn't worry me, I'm not ashamed of anybody or anything anymore.

Soon after, one of my English cousins came to see us. Her son had his bar mitzvah at the Temple David congregation, and Paul Vines, who had been a refugee from Austria, asked me to join the community. We did and became very active in Temple activities. Our children attended the Temple David Hebrew School and I taught Hebrew there.

We became friendly with the congregation rabbi, George Ruben. He was one of the Dunera boys. He'd lost his entire family in the Holocaust. He used to come to us every Shabbat and weekend. He was a very nice person but was something of a social misfit. He never spoke of his Dunera experience.

I'm a member of the National Council of Jewish Women and I've never been so happy in my life. I feel part of something, because I belong. People are really warm here but in Holland they seem unable to express this feeling.

After the war in Holland I think everybody was crazy, like we'd been thrown over a wall and nobody could get over what had happened. I was lucky to get out and come to Australia. There are many people here from everywhere. We have met and made friends with many of the migrants from different countries who tend to stick together, from England, Poland and many other places. I am a gregarious person and I love people. The Australian people are marvellous. Here, you get out of life what you put into it. I hold my head up high and speak my mind. I don't have to crawl in a corner because I'm a Jew, especially not here in Perth. We have returned to Holland a few times but the people are not the same, they seem to be different altogether.

This is my country. Here people are really wonderful. My parents never regretted my living in Australia. They could see for themselves that it was the best thing they ever did, encouraging me to migrate here. Without their encouragement I may not have come to Australia.

The Nazi experience had a considerable after-effect on my family in Holland and their attitude towards religion, and has split the family. My brother Lou and sister Sonja will have nothing to do with Judaism. My sister Sonja, who was taken to Westerbork, can't get it out of her system and says the Jewish people were not nice to her. Her daughter also has intense feelings about Judaism. My sister Ellen became ultra-religious after the war and wouldn't eat with her parents or brother and sisters. My father died a few years ago and was buried in a non-denominational section of the cemetery. Ellen and her children didn't like that and arranged for Father to be removed to an Orthodox Jewish burial ground. My brother and sister were very upset and this caused a further rift in the family.

My husband and I are very busy in our retirement. We do many things together. I make pottery and do spinning and weaving and teach craftwork sometimes. One thing I don't want to do is work with wood even though I was well trained in that field. I'm sorry I didn't finish my education. I tried kindergarten teaching but decided that my children were more important. I couldn't manage the time to finish the course.

Of course I have no regrets about leaving Holland, never. I'm free here.

§

Erica arrived in Perth with her son Martin in 1950, less than twelve months after the arrival of her husband, Klaas. They had no relatives in Australia and had to make a life for themselves independently. Two more children were born to them in Australia – Peter and Louise.

The 'house' Klaas bought on the property in Bedfordale was a very old building, and when she first saw it Erica reportedly exclaimed: 'What? I'm going to go back to Holland!' However, she stayed, and together she and Klaas worked hard to support their young family and make a success of their new lives in a new land.

For many years Erica would not talk about the war. Her son Martin was not aware of his mother's experiences, although he noticed that some things seemed to upset her and once saw her cry after seeing children playing with toy guns.

In 1990 Martin travelled to Holland and saw the names of Rebecca and Harold Deen etched into a war memorial in Loosdrecht. Martin began to research his mother's family, and uncovered information about thirty-five family members who were murdered in concentration camps.

*Erica (far right) with her son Martin (right) and family*

Martin talked to his mother about his discoveries and encouraged her to share her story. At first this was incredibly difficult for her, but she began, with tears in her eyes, to talk about her experiences. Eventually she was able to share her story with schoolchildren and with representatives from Steven Spielberg's Survivors of the Shoah Visual History Foundation, who recorded her testimony, and those of many survivors all over the world.

On 10 December 2013, those who risked their own lives to help save Erica during the war were officially recognised by Yad Vashem in Israel as Righteous Among the Nations at a ceremony in Amsterdam. Martin and his wife attended, with his son and daughter and six-year-old granddaughter Annabel. The Dutch families were represented by their descendants.

Erica lived a full and vibrant life in Perth. She was a farmer's wife, fighting bushfires, picking and

*The commemorative war memorial in Loosdrecht
bearing the names of Harold and Rebecca Deen, 1990*

packing fruit and vegetables and raising chickens. She was very skilled and practised many crafts including spinning, weaving and pottery. Erica travelled to Holland and Israel and was able to meet with some of those who had helped to protect her during the war, including Hans Sittig, who had driven her to her first place of refuge, and Hendrik and Mina Grootemarsink. In Australia, she looked after new immigrants from Holland and helped them to find work. In her spare time she enjoyed playing bridge. Erica passed

*Erica with her grandchildren*

away on 17 March 2014, a day after the birth of her twin great-grandchildren, one of whom is named after her.

*A version of Erica's narrative was originally published in the historical collection* Without Regret, *edited by Louise Hoffman and Shush Masel.*

## Kurt Ehrenfeld

I was born in Bratislava on 20 October 1932. The city I was born in was the capital of what was then the province of Slovakia, which was part of the Czechoslovak Republic. The city lies on the Danube River, about sixty kilometres downstream from Vienna. Bratislava is an old town; it has been there for many centuries. It is an attractive place, with many historic buildings. Slovakia was a largely Catholic country and there were many churches in the city. When I was born the population was about 150,000 and the Jewish community made up about ten per cent of this. There were other sizeable ethnic minorities including Hungarians and Germans. Bratislava was quite a cosmopolitan town. There was a fair concentration of Jewish families in the Jewish quarter, but those who were less religious, and so didn't need to live within walking distance of the shule, had become more scattered throughout the city. The Jews of Bratislava were typically middle-class – merchants and businessmen. There were also many professionals such as lawyers and doctors.

My father was named Oskar Ehrenfeld and he was born in 1903 in what was then the Austro-Hungarian Empire. My father was one of five children and his father Solomon Ehrenfeld was a merchant of some sort. His mother had died when he was quite young and he and his siblings were raised by his father. One of his sisters was sent to an orphanage. Their upbringing was not such a religious one. My paternal grandfather died when I was only a few months old.

My mother Esther (originally spelt 'Ester' and changed later when she moved to Australia) was born in 1900, into a very religious Orthodox family. Her father Solomon Weiler was a poultry shochet and ran a poultry business. Her mother had died when she and her sister were very young and her father remarried a woman named Leah. They went on to have another son and a daughter and Leah is the woman I knew as my grandmother. My maternal grandfather was a very religious man. He went three times a day to shule. On the festival of Sukkoth, he would build a little sukkah in the yard of his house. My maternal grandparents lived in the Jewish quarter of Bratislava, where Jews have lived for centuries.

My father held a senior position in a Slovakian bank. He started as a junior clerk and gradually rose to become an assistant manager of the bank. The apartment we rented in the downtown business district of Bratislava was owned by the bank and there was a branch downstairs in the same building. My father was

*Kurt's mother Esther Ehrenfeld*

a keen student, particularly of German literature and philosophy and our house was full of books – Goethe, Schiller, Nietzsche. My mother had been apprenticed as a seamstress and she ran her own dressmaking business from our home. My little sister Eva was born in 1934. The four of us lived together in our apartment, along with my aunt Katarina. We also had a woman who lived with us to help with the housework.

I remember celebrating Shabbat as a family. We would light the candles and my father would make Kiddush. We would visit my maternal grandparents for lunch on Saturdays, along with my uncles, aunts and cousins. We went to shule on the Jewish holidays and sometimes we would wander across and visit my grandfather in his more Orthodox shule. I don't remember much anti-Semitism before the war. There was the occasional taunting and teasing of Jews but before the war it wasn't too serious.

*Kurt with his mother*

There were a number of parochial government-supported schools in Bratislava, as well as two Jewish schools. One was very Orthodox, and my sister Eva and I attended the less Orthodox one. It was only about a ten-minute walk from our home. I remember a teacher called Mr Alt.

As a child I loved playing with Meccano sets. From a very early age I wanted to become a mechanical engineer. I also remember summer holidays at a spa in the countryside.

In 1938, the same year I started school, Hitler annexed Austria. Before the war we would occasionally travel to Vienna to visit my aunt there but this became impossible. When Hitler took over Austria the Sudetenland Germans living in Slovakia became very anti-Semitic and the strong Nazi party became very active in our country. My father's sister Iren and her

*Kurt with his father Oskar Ehrenfeld*

husband Kurt in Vienna realised that they were no longer safe living in Austria and tried to escape the country to travel to Palestine. They were captured by the British en route and were interned throughout the war in Mauritius.

In March 1939, German-occupied Czechoslovakia was ruled by a German military governor. Slovakia became a nominally independent puppet state and anti-Semitism became official policy.

When war broke out in September 1939 I was not quite seven years old. From that time on Jews became second-class citizens. Attacks on the street became more frequent. My parents became very anxious and depressed. They had lived through World War I as children and they could see another long war coming. They also knew that it was going to be difficult for the Jews. I remember standing on the balcony of our apartment and watching a demonstration on the street.

*Kurt and his sister Eva*

The crowd spotted us and yelled out, 'There's some Jews. Let's go and get them.' They came up to our flat and beat up my uncle and stole a few things. At other times Germans and Slovaks came to our apartment and stole things and pushed my father and uncle around.

Apart from the odd attack, the odd shoving on the street, life continued basically as before. Then more and more restrictions were introduced for Jews. You weren't allowed to walk along the Danube, you couldn't own land and Jewish businesses were expropriated. Jews couldn't go to the swimming pool or to the movies. No Jew could hold any senior position; they could not serve in the armed forces or with the police. My father was demoted from his position in the bank.

From 1940, Jews were no longer allowed to live anywhere they chose in Bratislava and were restricted to certain districts. Our family had to leave our home

*The Ehrenfeld family in 1941*

and move to a small apartment on Bastei Gasse in the Jewish quarter. We only had one room and a kitchen. Part of the kitchen was curtained off to make a bathroom. My aunt Katarina had married by this time and she and her husband shared a room in another apartment.

It wasn't a walled ghetto like Warsaw. Apart from the designated areas where Jews were not allowed to go, it was possible to move around the town. My father continued to go to work and I still went to school.

Jews were forbidden from owning radios, but our neighbours had them so we had some idea of what was happening in Europe. Nobody was allowed to listen to the BBC but people did so we heard some of the news about the war.

On Rosh Hashanah in 1941, all Jews had to commence wearing a yellow star. There were various shapes and sizes depending on your position. My father was still working at the bank so he was given quite a small star so it was not so obvious he was a Jew but the rest of us had to wear large stars on our outer clothing. They changed the pattern from time to time. We also had to carry special identity cards.

In the spring of 1942 the deportations of Jews to Auschwitz began. Among the first to go were the young women, girls from their late teens to early twenties. My cousin Herma Hirschler, who was the daughter of my mother's older sister, was sent to Auschwitz. She was a qualified secretary and was put to work in the camp working for the SS who kept meticulous records of all the people who were exterminated. Herma was in Auschwitz for three years and also survived a death march to Ravensbruck at the end of the war.

*Kurt's cousin Herma Hirschler, whose story is included in the book* Secretaries of Death: Accounts by Former Prisoners who worked in the Gestapo of Auschwitz *by Lore Shelley*

Next the young men were taken away. Herma's younger brother was sent to a camp. Her older brother was spared because he was conscripted into a labour battalion attached to the Slovak army. He later escaped and joined the Partisans.

Over the year they came with lists of people to deport. All of my family members were rounded up and sent to camps. My grandparents were sent to Auschwitz. They were old people; we knew they would have been sent straight to the gas chambers. My mother had somehow been able to arrange to see them at the collection camp where they were held before being transported to Auschwitz. She came back crying and very upset. She didn't tell me until years later, but my grandfather had said to her, 'Don't worry – I'm over seventy. I've had my three score years and ten and I'm ready to go if that's what God wants.'

My father was classified as an 'economically important Jew' and we were not deported with the rest of the community. Only about fifteen per cent of the Jews of Bratislava remained after the deportations of 1942. Our school closed and the small number of children and teachers who were left were put into a makeshift school. Officially Jews were not allowed to be taught advanced subjects but our teachers did what they could to maintain educational standards.

Once the first wave of deportations in 1942 was over there was a relatively quiet period and persecution abated for a while. The German army had been pretty comprehensively beaten at Stalingrad by that time. The Slovaks had started to become a bit jittery – perhaps they thought that just maybe they had picked the wrong side. Of course no one could say this too loudly as the

*Kurt and sister Eva with their father in 1943, bank in background*

*Kurt (front row, second left) and his class in the makeshift Jewish school, 1943*

Germans were still in control but there was a definite change of scenery in 1943.

My father knew that the Germans were not going to give up and he arranged for us to become Hungarian

*Kurt in 1943*

citizens to protect us – this was possible because both my parents had been born in the old Austro-Hungarian Empire. We were issued with new passports. This had certain advantages as the Jews of Hungary were relatively unscathed at that time. As Hungarian citizens we didn't have to wear the yellow star anymore. We all kept low profiles and life continued – until the Germans occupied Hungary and began to deport the Hungarian Jews to the camps. It was no longer advantageous to be a Hungarian citizen.

My father began to arrange for some potential hiding places for us. We knew what was going on; rumours of the gas chambers had begun to circulate. My cousin Herma was able to send out some letters from Auschwitz. Of course they were heavily censored but we could understand the messages between the lines. She would write things like, 'Uncle Freddy is here together with Joe Grunewald.' Joe

Grunewald had died some years ago so we knew what the situation was.

Our lives became more and more difficult, however, with many restrictions in place. Our country was now being bombed by the Allies but Jews were not allowed to go into the air-raid shelters to escape the bombing. My father could see the writing on the wall and began to make plans for us to go into hiding when the time came to try and escape. He was fortunate because he had non-Jewish contacts through his work at the bank and was also friendly with the general manager.

We were in a little backwater of Europe which was temporarily out of the limelight because the Germans had bigger fish to fry, but we were aware that this would not last, that we would not be left in peace.

There was a non-Jewish woman called Mara who had been our daily help. She was a widow in her fifties and a very nice person. My father was able to acquire a house in her name in the outer suburbs. It was up in the hills with only a walking path to the house and a large cellar, which would be a good hiding place. He also managed to get another apartment in the name of another woman called Yana. He knew that when we did have to go into hiding we may need to move around.

We continued to live in our own apartment until August 1944 when there was an uprising in Slovakia against the Nazis. This caused the Germans to move their army into Slovakia. A large number of German troops arrived and with them they brought the SS and all the other apparatus. We knew that our time was up and we decided to go into hiding at Yana's place.

We couldn't take suitcases as that would have been too conspicuous so we just had our basic things with us. We just walked down the street casually and into the apartment. We had to be very quiet. Throughout this time in hiding my father continued to go to work. One day the rest of us looked out of the apartment window and saw crowds of Jews with suitcases being led up the street. We knew that there had been a round-up of all the Jews. My mother said then that if my father had been caught and did not come back then we would all give ourselves up too.

A Jewish friend called Olga came to the apartment. They had come to deport her and she only took a shopping bag. As they marched past the markets she had slipped away. She only had a small bag so she looked like an ordinary housefrau doing her shopping. My father eventually came back. Someone at work had seen him and warned him and told him that he should hide. He sent Olga to hide at Mara's house in the hills.

My Aunt Katarina and her husband had been in their flat when they came to round them up. They sat in their room very quietly and somehow the Germans never opened the door and found them. They took the train to Mara's place and hid there too. All the people who were in hiding at Mara's place managed to survive until the Russians came.

Mara pretended that she was a charlady working for Yana so that she had a legitimate reason to come and bring supplies for us. She would tell stories about how fussy Yana was and how she had to spend hours cleaning. Yana was well paid to hide us but one day there was a typewritten letter in her letterbox. It said, 'We know you are hiding Jews. Get rid of them or we will denounce you.' The letter was signed simply

'Neighbours', there was no signature. We do not know who sent that letter or why.

We moved to another apartment owned by a couple called Mr and Mrs Rosa. My father must have prearranged it for us. There were two other young Jewish women hiding there. Their husbands had been taken away. We had to be very quiet and if there was an air raid we couldn't go to the shelter with everyone else. We had to be careful even when we were using the toilet in case someone heard us.

One day Mr Rosa came home in the company of a Gestapo man and he told us to pack up and go with him. We don't know who betrayed us. We think perhaps the people who were hiding us wanted to get hold of some of our possessions and they denounced us so we would just disappear.

The Gestapo man took all six of us away in a taxi, which my father had to pay for, to a school which they used to gather Jews who had been caught. My father was interrogated there but he wasn't physically harmed. There were quite a few Jews there. We stayed there for two or three days and then were taken by truck to a railway station.

We were taken to Sered, which was a collection camp in the Slovak countryside. It was basically just wooden barracks and large dormitories and was fenced and guarded. There were a lot of elderly people there and I remember an old lady in her seventies in the bunk next to us saying, 'You are young, you will survive, but I won't.' We were kept there for about a month and two young women conducted classes for the children.

One day in mid-December 1944 we were told to

get our things and line up. We were put into lines and shuffled before an SS officer. His job was to select those who could work and those who could not. He pointed to me and asked my father: 'Is he a strong boy?' 'No, he's not,' said my father, 'he's weak.' So my father was sent in one direction and my mother and sister and I in another. That was the last I ever saw of my father.

There were SS men with submachine guns patrolling the perimeter of the camp. I remember thinking: 'Why are they carrying machine guns? We are not in a position to do anything to them.'

A group of about eighty women and children were put into a cattle car. It was midwinter in Europe and very cold. Box cars are not designed to carry eighty people. There were no toilets. We all just huddled together and they closed the door and the train took off. The train stopped at numerous stations and was recoupled. The railway workers continued like it was just another freight train. They would check the train at each station and check the tyres by hitting them with a sledgehammer. There were two tiny windows and I remember one young woman calling out in Slovak, 'Where are we?' They told her the name of the village. They system just continued to roll. Eichmann's system.

I would try to figure out where we were going from the direction of the sun. We were concerned that we would be taken to Auschwitz although we knew that the Russians were close to Auschwitz so maybe we would be spared. I concluded that we were basically travelling westwards.

After about four days we eventually stopped at a railway siding and were told to get off. We were at Theresienstadt. There were Jewish women who had been in the camp for some time and worked as assistants. One of them gave me a cup of water – it was such a marvellous experience.

My mother and sister were sent to one part of the camp and all the boys to another part. We had showers and our heads were shaved. We continued to wear our own clothes, not a uniform. Theresienstadt was classified as a ghetto, not a concentration camp. It had been a garrison town in earlier times and there were a lot of military barracks so it was considered suitable for camp accommodation. The non-Jewish population had been relocated out of the town.

We were put into barracks while waiting to be sorted. Many of the older people who had travelled with us died soon after their arrival at Theresienstadt. This was the first time I had come across deceased bodies. They were piled up on carts and wheeled away. The old lady we had met in Sered died within a few days of arriving at the camp.

From the barracks, my sister Eva was put into a dormitory for girls and I was put in one with triple bunks in the section for boys. Within the ghetto we could walk around and my mother would come to visit us.

There were around fifteen thousand Jews left in Theresienstadt. The women who had met us at the trains told us that a short while earlier there had been up to fifty or sixty thousand but they had all been transported to the camps and only those required to run the place remained behind. They told us that before too long the transports would resume again but it never happened because the front was just too close.

When we had been at Theresienstadt for a couple of months, I became ill with severe jaundice and was put into hospital where they tried to treat me with what limited medication was available. I stayed there for several weeks and when I was discharged I was allowed to stay with my mother. This was in early April of 1945.

We knew by then that the front was approaching. You could see the vapour trails of the bombers. There were no more deportations. Actually the opposite started to happen as the front approached and the Nazis evacuated the concentration camps and started the forced marches of prisoners to Theresienstadt.

My mother's dormitory was near the railway siding and I could see the prisoners arriving. They were wearing striped pyjamas and were in very poor condition. We looked for my father among them. Others prisoners were brought on trains. They would write the number of people in chalk on the side of the wagon. As they died they would just change the number; eighty-seven, eighty-six, eighty-five. People from Theresienstadt would have to come and take the dead bodies away on carts. I was watching all this from my mother's window and a Czech gendarme saw me and waved me away.

When we saw these people from the camps arriving we wanted to feed them but the doctors told us, 'We must be very careful about how we bring them back.' So many of them died there. The war was nearly over, the Germans were bringing people there because no doubt they had plans to wipe us all out but events just moved too quickly for them.

One evening around the seventh of May a Slovak boy came and told us, 'The Russians are here!' Some people didn't believe it and thought that it was just a ruse but the following day we saw thousands of Russian troops moving past towards Prague. Germany had already surrendered.

It was over. My sister and mother and I were alive. My father never came back.

One of my cousins who had survived had gone to the Red Cross in Bratislava and looked up our names on the lists of survivors. He came to Theresienstadt and escorted us back to Bratislava. The town hadn't changed that much; it had sustained some damage but not too much.

We went up to Mara's place in the hills and stayed there. My aunt was there. We waited for my father and visited all the old places. I now know how people look when they have seen a ghost. When my sister and I would walk into a room people were amazed. 'We thought you were dead,' they told us.

The general population was not friendly to us. The Catholic priests used to preach about how terrible the Jews were, how they had killed Christ. There are very few Jews left in Slovakia.

It was pure fluke that we had survived. That and my father's foresight in arranging hiding places so that we survived long enough to avoid being sent to Auschwitz.

I think that humanity works in strange ways. The people who rise to power are not necessarily the ones who are best qualified to lead the people to a better place. Quite often it's the lunatics who rise to power. This is why there have been so many evil empires throughout history. The Nazi regime was one but there have been others since and there may be more in the future. If I have a message it is this: be on your guard.

§

*Kurt, Herma, Esther and Eva after the war*

The country that Kurt and his mother and sister returned to was mostly empty of its Jewish community. According to data gathered by Yad Vashem, around 100,000 Slovakian Jews were murdered by the Germans, with an estimated twenty-five thousand to thirty-five thousand surviving the camps or escaping death by remaining hidden.

Kurt's mother Esther was able to recover some of the family's possessions that had been stored with friends and also found a small apartment to rent on Bastei Gasse – the same street in the Jewish quarter where the family had lived during the war. Esther searched desperately for news of her husband and eventually discovered that he had died in Bergen-Belsen. Nearly all of Kurt's extended family, as well as most of the Jews of Bratislava, had been killed.

Kurt and his younger sister Eva returned to school after missing out on so much of their education. Kurt was a gifted student and received outstanding results.

*Eva, Esther and Kurt Ehrenfeld in 1947*

He also attended classes in Jewish education in preparation for his bar mitzvah with a private tutor. He celebrated his bar mitzvah in one of the old shules that had been reopened after the war.

Kurt and Eva both joined a Jewish youth movement in Slovakia and began to embrace Zionism, especially after the state of Israel was established as the Jewish homeland in 1948. By that time Slovakia was under Communist rule and most of the remaining Jews decided to leave the country. The Communist government gave permission for Jewish citizens to emigrate to Israel. Many Slovak Jews claimed to be leaving for Israel but instead travelled only as far as Vienna and then on to other destinations. Kurt's mother Esther suffered significant health problems after her wartime experience and was reluctant to migrate to the fledgling nation of Israel. However, Kurt and Eva, both teenagers by this time, were full of enthusiasm for a new life in the Jewish homeland. When the family arrived in Israel in 1949, Kurt went to live on a kibbutz called Nirim in the Negev desert. Eva was sent to a different kibbutz and Esther settled in the city of Haifa.

The Ehrenfelds did not remain in Israel for long. Suffering from a heart ailment, Esther found the climate extremely challenging and made arrangements to return to Europe. Esther, Kurt and Eva returned to Vienna, where they lived for a year while waiting for an immigration permit to Australia. Esther sold some pieces of her remaining jewellery to support the family. Kurt and Eva took English classes in preparation for their move to Australia.

In 1950 Esther, Kurt and Eva travelled to Melbourne on an Italian ship named *Surriento*. The Ehrenfelds rented a room from a family in Elwood, later renting a small house in East Brunswick and then another apartment in Elwood. Kurt found work at the T&G Insurance office but he was still determined to fulfil his dream of becoming an engineer so enrolled in a mechanical engineering course at RMIT.

Eva married Charlie Migdalek in August 1953. A few weeks later Esther passed away. After the death of their mother, Kurt lived with with Eva and Charlie, continuing with his study until he eventually graduated as an engineer and found a job as a draftsman at an engineering firm.

Kurt met his future wife Norma Lore on the St Kilda tram. Norma's parents were born in Safed in Palestine but had migrated to Perth, where she was born. After she completed her schooling, Norma had moved to Melbourne in search of a more cosmopolitan and exciting lifestyle. Kurt and Norma were married in January 1958. In 1959 the couple welcomed their first son, Jeffrey.

*Kurt and Norma with four of their sons*

At this stage they decided to move back to Perth to be near Norma's family. They lived with their young baby for several months with Norma's parents until they were able to purchase their own home in Bradford Street, Menora. The Ehrenfelds went on to have five more sons – Danny, Gabriel, Leon, Miron and Simon. A daughter named Natanya followed the six boys.

Kurt found work with the Public Works Department on the Ord River Project and then went on to establish a successful career as a consultant engineer. The family built a home on Pine Street in Menora, where they have lived for several decades.

Kurt and Norma presided over a close-knit, loving family, welcoming twelve grandchildren over the years. In 2007 Kurt travelled back to Bratislava and walked through the streets of his childhood for the first time in nearly half a century.

Kurt passed away on 1 July 2014.

# Anonymous

When I was a little girl my mother told me that every child has an angel and that my angel would guide me through my life. Of course I knew that angel was my mother. So I am alive today and Hitler has been buried for seventy years. He cast a death sentence on me as he did millions of others, but what he did not know was that he did not know my mother!

Hitler was a great coward. He built himself a nest in Berchtesgaden in the Austrian mountains called Eagle's Nest. There was not a bomb at the time that could destroy the granite mountain. He was insensitive to the destruction of his own country and when the Russians were advancing on Berlin most of his soldiers were dead or wounded so at his command boys as young as twelve or thirteen were standing up to the Russian army.

What I remember: the beauty of the country I was born in – Poland. The enormous forests. Some of the cities were named after trees. Sosnowiec from the word *sosna* for pine tree. Dombrowa after the forests of oak trees. Oberschlesien, the German border, was on one side and the Polish/Czech alps on the other.

I was born in Chorzow, which was firstly German and then became Polish, so there remained a German influence in the town. There, Germans who stayed and did not retreat were called *Volksdeutsche*.

We lived in a two-storey building and I remember vividly the *Volksdeutsche* engineer and his family who lived next door. As a child I loved going to their place. His hobby was winemaking and in his enormous high-ceilinged kitchen were glass jars and a network of tubes filled with red wine. I was fascinated.

Our neighbours invited us in at Christmas to see their Christmas tree. As a child I remember being enthralled and gazing at it in wonder. From a child's viewpoint it was so beautiful. Each day a sparkler was lit. As you can imagine, I was very little and it seemed so romantic and colourful.

We of course celebrated Hanukkah. My father had inherited his great-grandfather's menorah and each day another wick was lit. I remember that there were two lions engraved on it – the lions of Judah. However, from my viewpoint as a small child it did somehow seem quite simple and lacked the colour and romance of that Christmas tree next door!

My father was a company accountant and was in charge of the accounts department. He worked for a couple called the Furstenbergs who employed two thousand people. The Furstenbergs were philanthropists. They built a Jewish school, both a primary school and a high school called Yavne. The building was in the Roman style with pillars and was quite beautiful. My sister and I went to that school. The teachers were highly qualified and taught Latin, Hebrew, Polish and German. However, the Furstenbergs were not totally philanthropic! My father, as the accountant, kept a record of the overtime all the workers did and eventually he took the firm to court for underpaying them.

I remember my father being a man of kindness and principle. Once a painter had no shoes so my father took his off and gave them to the worker. He was also a man who loved learning and was a great reader at a time when books were leatherbound and so very expensive. Mother would complain that she could do with more money for housekeeping! He read Goethe, Pushkin and Tolstoy and he could speak Russian, Polish, Hebrew and German.

Father would take my sister and me out on Sundays to a castle on a hill a bit like Kings Park. It was not too far to go. On a Sunday there would be an orchestra, just brass. I remember it being a beautiful outing in the summer. There would be families and children and couples here and there enjoying a little romance. It remains in my memory as a very happy occasion.

Other Sundays Father would take my sister and me into the fields. I remember the storks and how we were told if we made a wish it would come true. So I did a little dance and asked the stork for a baby brother. Soon after a baby was born to our neighbours on the second floor of our apartment building and I was told that the stork had brought the baby. I went outside and looked up at their apartment. All the windows were closed and no glass was broken. I went back inside and said to my mother that the stork could not possibly have brought the baby. After that there was much whispering and laughter.

I had just had my thirteenth birthday when war broke out. I remember the build-up. Father was reading the paper and I would see the cartoons. They depicted Jewish people with enormous stomachs and hooked noses. In front of them were drawn little victims. Something was communicated to me although I was only a child and did not understand.

German Jews were expelled from Germany. They came to Poland destitute. Hitler marched into Poland in September 1939. And there they were.

Germany was a highly cultured country. They produced Goethe and Wagner. By 1939 they were already very high-tech. They had planes called Stukas that could dive down and kill people and then ascend just like a helicopter. They also had von Braun working on a rocket that was intended for London.

My mother, sister and I were walking in the street when the highly developed Stukas came down firing indiscriminately. This was our introduction to the German presence in Poland. They attacked on Hitler's orders. From that moment, I recall the saying 'the dead are better off than the living'.

The Germans set the synagogue alight. They locked the doors and set fire to it. The people were burnt to death inside. To stir anger and prejudice the Germans showed pictures of the most unlikely people – Ultra-Orthodox Jews – attacking Germans!

My father and my mother had to make the greatest decision of their lives. My father had a mother who was frail and old, but my mother was determined to try to cross the Russian border, believing that we would be safe. My father stayed behind with his mother as she was incapable of travel.

My mother, sister and I left by train for the Russian border. We came to a beautiful town called Zamosc close to Russia. In a few days we were supposed to cross the border. However, disastrous news came. The number of German guards had increased – along with their Alsatian dogs. Whoever came near would be shot on the spot or attacked by the dogs. Mother had a dilemma – what do to? It was now too risky to attempt to cross the border, so we stayed on in Zamosc. There we were recruited for *zwangsarbeit* (forced labour). The work was in the fields, planting or harvesting potatoes, strawberries and other crops.

My sister and I worked in different fields, and my mother in another. I remember there was always a parcel with bread or some other food left where my sister worked. The parcels were left by a German solider who would come to the fence and leave bread for my sister. It was the first time I had experienced that there were good people in the world. That bread played a big part in our diet thanks to that unknown soldier. This went on until October 1942.

I recall that it was the coldest winter on record. German tanks were driving into Russia. The men were dressed only in flimsy clothing and the petrol froze in their tanks. The German army, so ill-prepared and ill-equipped for a Russian winter, was humiliated and defeated on the Russian front. At this point Hitler came up with his 'final solution' for the Jews. The ghetto, which all the Jews had been forced into some time earlier, was liquidated.

Then came a day imprinted on my memory. I couldn't go to work as I felt sick. I heard German voices and boots. I jumped into a cupboard and closed the door. These men were in full uniform with belts, guns and bullets. Mother's angel came: they were looking for people, scooping them up to put on the train – but they didn't find me.

A few days later they came and ordered everyone out into the city square. My mother, sister and I, along with hundreds of others young, old and frail, were mercilessly made to march. We marched for about twenty kilometres to a little township and there we stopped. Cattle trains were lined up at the station. Some of the wagons were already occupied and I could hear the mourning and wailing coming from inside.

As we stopped marching and were able to relax a little, we walked around and there we met a Polish friend, a Christian girl from Zamosc. She told us that an *akcja* (action), the gathering of everyone by the Germans, was going to happen. She said that she had a small wooden shed behind her house where we could hide while the Germans were rounding people up. By then it was just my mother and me as we were minus my sister. I discovered later that my mother had encouraged my sister to disappear into a tall field of corn while we were marching.

Inside the storeroom there was a big pile of chopped wood. We managed to crawl under the wood. I remember my mother being in pain with a shocking backache. I also clearly remember thinking, 'If I ever survive, I will never, ever have children!'

While we were hiding under the wood, we heard the padlock beginning to rattle. Germans! Then we heard the voice of our friend. 'What are you doing?' she asked them. 'There is only wood in there.' The Germans left without searching.

Sometime later when we came out of the woodshed, my mother took me by the hand and led me away from the cattle trucks to the railway station. Our friend in Zamosc had told my mother that a friend of hers lived in Drohobycz and might be able to help us. My mother gave me the address and some money. She hugged me and kissed me and put me on the train.

I never saw my mother again, just as I never saw my father again.

I remember that I was wearing a polka-dotted blue headscarf knotted under my chin. In the train compartment with me was a couple, who sat next to me. After a time, the man flicked his lighter to light a cigarette. As the flame sprang to life, my face was illuminated. He saw my face and my eyes, which must have told the whole story. He just said *zydowka*, which means Jewess. That was all he said – no more.

I arrived in Drohobycz and found the address my mother had given me. The family let me in. I remember that there were four children and they were quite religious Catholics. Their father had been killed. I stayed with them for one week. In that week the Germans began a large *akcja* and started rounding up all the Jewish people, putting them on cattle trains. I knew that the Germans would punish the family if they were found to be hiding me.

One night I had a dream. It was so real that I felt as if my mother were with me, by my side. She spoke to me. She said, 'Take off the Star of David.' Then she led me by the hand. We were in our home town. She took me through the underpass near the factory and the city. Every day I had walked through that underpass to the city and to school. My mother led me through the underpass and out into the open and then she disappeared.

The vivid dream of my mother had been so real that I cried. I didn't want the family to see me crying so I turned away from them and faced the window. As I did so, I saw fully armed Germans – they were either SS men or Gestapo – open the gate and walk towards the house. I went into the kitchen to raise the alarm. I called to the family: 'Germans are coming!' The two older children and I ran into the yard and hid in the shed. The mother and the two younger ones remained in the house.

After the soldiers left we came out of hiding and returned to the house. The Germans had conscripted one of the younger girls, who was about fourteen years old, and registered her as a slave labourer to work in Germany. She had to report for duty in three days. It was then that the mother asked me, 'Would you like to go instead of Yadwiga and take her name?' We were both about the same age and so there was a similarity. The children's mother then went to the church and brought back some holy water. She said that 'Maria' would look after me.

I remembered my mother and thought, 'I have my angel.' I had three days to prepare to leave. I was now Yadwiga Trybuch.

The time came to leave and I went to the railway station, which was the gathering point for Poles who had been conscripted for slave labour in Germany. As we were all gathered together and directed to enter the cattle wagons, a girl came up to me, introduced herself and asked me my name. 'I am Yadwiga Trybuch,' I told her. She answered: 'I am a longstanding schoolfriend of Yadwiga's.' My heart felt as if it had stopped beating for a moment. I looked around to see if a finger was pointed at me. Would a German come to take me away? Nothing happened. No fingers pointed. No one came. I felt my angel guarding me.

I do not remember the name of the city we stopped at next. I do remember the huge barracks where they gathered all the so-called 'slave labourers' on their way to Germany. We slept in bunk beds in an enormous hall. When we arrived lots of young people were already there – mostly young girls. A group of youngsters dressed in Polish national costumes was dancing a national dance. Then there was silence. Two SS men arrived. They picked a beautiful girl from the dance group and took her away. A murmur spread through the silence. *Jewess*. Again my heart felt as if it missed a beat, but my angel revived me.

We spent a few days at the barracks waiting to be dispersed to different parts of Germany to replace the men who were fighting in the war.

On the second day something happened that has remained etched in my memory. I had a lower bunk. Coming from the bunk above me I heard rhythmic bumps. As they got louder, the lights in the dormitory went on and everyone's attention became drawn to my bunk. The top bunk was occupied by a Polish girl who obviously did not want to go to Germany. She had torn her blouse into shreds and tied her hair in knots. In her hand she had a small metal saucepan which she was using to repeatedly knock herself on the head.

I shrivelled up with fear. I crawled out from my bunk and went outside into the cold and the snow. I took a few steps and then I blacked out. I just fell to the ground. I don't know how long I was lying in the snow, but when I finally got up my clothes were drenched and I was shivering with cold. I went back to my bunk. The Polish girl upstairs was escorted away by two SS men.

Not long after that the trains arrived to transport us to our destination. We were loaded into the wagons from the journey to a town called Eisfeld in Thuringen. It was a very long journey. I remember sometimes not responding when someone called me 'Wishia', which is a pet name for Yadwiga. Even worse, the girls began to sing a religious song about the sunrise and God, meaning Jesus Christ, and I said rather stupidly and without thinking, 'I don't know that song.' There was silence. But my angel was with me. Finally we arrived in Germany.

Immediately upon arrival we were put through the dehumanising process of delousing and disinfecting before being assigned to yet another barracks filled with bunk beds. This time I made claim to a top bunk and there I lived for three years – from 1942 to 1945 – with fifteen Polish girls.

We were assigned to work in the Brunwerke factory in the city of Eisfeld. It was a lovely city. I remember the beautiful gardens and espaliered apple trees – 'normality', but definitely in inverted commas for me.

Every day we walked from the barracks to the Brunwerke factory and at lunchtime we were served two potatoes and soup. The canisters of soup were transported on a little wagon driven by an Italian prisoner of war. I always knew when he was coming because he would sing in his beautiful tenor voice the song 'Mamma, Son Tanto Felice'. The lines in the song meant, 'My dear mother, when will I return to you?'

In 1943 Germany was cut up, but it was like a snake – even when cut to pieces it still pulsed with life. Then came the bombings. Naturally our barracks were built near the railway station. On some nights the sky would light up. A 'Christmas tree' of lights came down from the planes lighting up the area to give the Allies an idea of where to bomb.

One night I was lying on the ground and thinking to myself, 'I am God's creation. I am a human, so I can't dig and burrow into the earth. I am above the animal world, but what is this going on all around me. Is this humanity?'

Some of the Allied planes were shot down and the pilots parachuted to earth and were captured and taken away as prisoners of war. Finally one day we heard the Italian prisoners of war singing. They were marching with torches. That was the day that Rommel was defeated by the British in Africa. Before that the Germans were also defeated in Russia.

Finally I remember, when it was all over, a Ukrainian man who had also been a slave labourer living in barracks near mine said to me, 'We knew. But we didn't want to give you away.' Ukrainians were known to come from a background that cooperated with the Nazis. This man, and probably everyone else, had known that I was Jewish but for some reason no one betrayed me.

The Americans entered Eisfeld in April 1945. We saw the tanks coming. The best day of my life. I had such a feeling of gratitude. These days America is often depicted as the 'big Satan', but I know how wrong that judgement is. The American liberating army was so civilised. There was no retribution and a lot of understanding and tolerance. The soldiers and the officers looked very similar and it was hard to differentiate between them. Sadly the American occupation did not last long. Unfortunately the Russians had marched into Berlin first and so occupied the capital of Germany. The Allies (America, France and the United Kingdom) felt that they needed to gain access to Berlin and so they made a deal in which they gained part of Berlin in exchange for Thuringen. So by July 1945 the Americans were replaced by the Russian army.

How very different the Russians were. Firstly the officers were dressed in their finery, sporting medals and looking and acting like peacocks. In contrast, the ordinary soldiers were more like bedraggled barbarians. I remember that they ate their food from a large copper stew pot. There seemed to be no discipline and they embarked on an orgy of rape and reprisals. It was so bad that we had to go into hiding for a week.

Things then began to settle down and we started to look for a train to take us out of Germany and back to Poland. Meanwhile, the Russians had been busy dismantling the German armaments that the factories were making in order to take them back to Russia. So when our train came we shared it not only with a crowd of refugees, but also whole factories of dismantled German military equipment bound for Russia. On the train there were lots of other refugees like us, both young and old, all speaking different languages.

Finally the train arrived in Poland and we disembarked in Katowice. My very first impression? A Polish girl saw me and said, 'Look at that Jewish girl across the road. What a shame Hitler didn't finish them off.'

Later my friend and I were found by a Jewish man who had been sent from Palestine to make contact with survivors and bring them back to the Jewish homeland. At that time it was illegal, because the state of Israel had not yet been declared and Palestine was still under the British mandate, so we were instructed that on the first part of our journey over the mountains to Salzburg, we were to be presented as a group of deaf and dumb children who were being escorted somewhere to get assistance with their disabilities.

We set off and climbed the mountains of Austria on a carefully planned route until we finally arrived in Salzburg and stayed in a displaced persons camp. Our group leader had to go to Munich to get instructions about the journey to Palestine. In Munich at that time people were discussing who they had met and where they were, always hoping to reunite families. When the group leader came back he brought me some very good news. My sister was alive!

This was the most beautiful moment of my life. I had a premonition that somehow she would survive. I left the group in Salzburg and went to see my sister who was in Regensburg in Germany. My sister went to Israel first and I followed later.

Meanwhile, little did I know but my guardian angel was working full-time 'down under'. The man that would become my husband was coming to Israel from Australia to visit his pioneering family there. When we met I asked him if he came on a white horse. He answered that actually he had come on a donkey!

We got married, for better and for worse, in sickness and in health, and I broke my promise to myself to not ever have children. It is the best promise I have ever broken and we are blessed to have two beautiful sons and two grandsons who are a joy to us.

When we go to Israel we visit the memorial in Modiin for all the Jews of the Zaglebie region of southwest Poland who perished in the Holocaust. There is a memorial forest with a stone marker for each different village. My father's and mother's names are engraved in Hebrew in the black stone and when I read my mother's name, I go back to my wonderful childhood memories. Her ability to create a happy, loving atmosphere of beauty and love in our home stays with me to this day. My mother, my guardian angel.

# Chaim Majteles

I was born in 1925 in a small town in south-west Poland, not far from the border with Germany. My parents were fairly prosperous. They owned a shoe retailing business as well as a small shoe factory. Ours was a contented home. I attended a school in which I was the only Jewish boy in a class of sixty. I was a fairly good student. I dreamed of becoming a doctor, but my father insisted I leave school and enter the family business.

After Hitler came to power in Germany in 1933, anti-Jewish feeling intensified among the local non-Jewish population. My uncle, who had always dreamed of living in Israel, took this as his cue to leave Poland. He begged my parents to join him but my father decided to stay.

With the invasion of Poland in September 1939, everything changed. Decrees appeared in the form of

*The only surviving photograph of Chaim's family before the war, taken in 1936. Chaim is on the far right.*

posters, pasted on walls everywhere. Goods like food, petrol, cigarettes and liquor became rationed. Queues formed outside shops as panic buying began. Polish currency was replaced by German marks. Our savings became worthless overnight. All citizens were issued identity cards and ration cards. We Jews had a different colour identity card and a large 'J' stamped on our ration cards. We were given smaller food rations and many more restrictions were placed on us. As well, we were required to wear white armbands with a blue Star of David. There were severe penalties for failing to comply.

There were frequent manhunts in our district to round up Jewish labourers for deportation to Germany. My parents managed to obtain special identity cards, at great sacrifice, to exempt us from deportation. In the spring of 1940, when I was fifteen, our possessions were confiscated. We were forced into a ghetto in a larger nearby town. Conditions in the ghetto were deplorable. Food and medicines were scarce. We received barely enough food to keep us alive. My brother and I worked in a nearby shoe factory, repairing military boots which had been collected from dead or wounded German soldiers. We were regarded as 'useful'. Others were not so fortunate and were subject to raids for deportation. These would occur at any time, day or night. People were rounded up and handed over to the Gestapo. We heard stories of their fate but didn't want to believe them.

One day in September 1942, all the Jews in the ghetto were forced to assemble in the ghetto square. Several selection points had been set up around the square. As we approached our selection point, the SS guards forcibly tore my family apart. Everything happened so fast that we did not even have time to say goodbye to each other. My older brother and I were released, but my parents, my sister Faye and my little brother Sam were forced into a barbed wire enclosure not far from the nearby railway siding where cattle trucks were waiting to be loaded. I began to cry. Then I remembered that I had managed to keep hidden some of my mother's jewellery. I bribed a guard to release my family. I found my father, but others were lost in an enormous milling mass of people. I last saw them being loaded onto the train and watched it disappear into the distance. This was the worst moment of my life.

Nineteen forty-two had been difficult, but in 1943 it became even harder to survive. The SS skilfully fed rumours into the ghetto that only a portion of the Jews would be required for deportation. They sold the Jewish leaders the line that maximum cooperation would give the best chance of survival. Even as the ghetto was gradually emptying, people were desperately trying to make themselves indispensable to the Germans. They were reluctant to believe in the existence of extermination camps.

The liquidation of the ghetto finally started in May 1943, a few days after my eighteenth birthday. Only those with certain skills were resettled in Srodula, a suburb of the nearby larger town of Sosnowiec. My father, my brother and I were relieved to find our names on the list of 'useful Jews'.

The Srodula ghetto was like a prison, with barbed wire fences and guarded by the SS troops in watchtowers. We lived in a crowded apartment with two other families. Every move we made was watched by the guards. Unbelievably, some people managed to escape, but their freedom was usually short-lived. Certain hostile Poles helped the Nazis hunt them down in return for a kilo of sugar or a bottle of vodka.

The Srodula ghetto was liquidated in autumn 1943. I was hiding in a bunker with my father during the round-up, but my brother was caught and deported. During a mopping-up operation several days later, my father and I were discovered. We were forced into a column with others who had previously evaded capture. We were marched under guard to the cattle wagons. There I witnessed dreadful scenes, as guards picked up small babies by their feet and swung them against the edge of the rail wagons, splitting their heads open while their parents watched helplessly.

We were packed into wagons so tightly that there was barely enough room to sit on the floor. High up on the carriage wall was a small opening to enable us to breathe. I was quite sure that at the end of our journey, we were all going to die.

I decided to try and escape. I made my peace with my father. He gave me several gold coins, which I hid in the heel of my shoe. With his help, I climbed up to the small opening. There were guards on top of each carriage. As we passed through a thick forest, I was pushed through the opening and jumped from the train. The guards opened fire and I was hit in the left wrist. I pressed myself flat against the ground. I knew that they would come looking for me with dogs so I had to get away as quickly as possible. Wrapping my hand in a handkerchief, I removed my Star of David and headed back towards Srodula. I reckoned that the Germans would least expect to find me heading in that direction.

When I reached the ghetto, I found that the remnants of the ghetto population were being used to remove household items and furniture from the empty dwellings. Security was lax compared with that which existed previously.

I joined a work party and was befriended by one of the workers, Herman Weissalz. He took me under his wing and arranged for the bullet to be removed from my wrist. During the next few months, there were repeated selections. With less than a hundred of us left, we knew time was running out. Herman managed to arrange for us to be hidden out in a village not far from Sosnowiec. We escaped after bribing a guard. This was now November 1943.

There were seven of us hidden in a bunker in the cellar of the farmhouse. A kerosene lamp on the wall provided the only light. There was straw strewn on the floor. Life in this hide-out was very dull. At the same time, we were terrified of discovery. The owner of the farm was being paid to hide us. However, he was openly hostile and would beat his wife if she gave us more than a meagre supply of food.

Contacts with the local population were used to furnish me with false papers. Using these, I was able to obtain extra rations regularly. On my return from one of these sorties, I found that a trap had been laid for me by the farmer. He had intended to kill me. It was obvious that it would not be long before we were turned out of his home.

We decided to try and escape to Rumania. It was necessary for me to contact a smuggler in Zwardon, near the border of Czechoslovakia. At Zwardon railway station, uniformed police were checking all passengers, looking for army deserters. My identity papers were checked and found to be false. After a brutal interrogation, it was clear that I was believed to be an army deserter and sentenced to death. The only way to avoid execution was to convince them that I was a Jew.

It was on 11 May 1944, two days after my nineteenth birthday, that I finally arrived in Auschwitz. Fortunately, I was not selected for immediate execution. The number 187818 was tattooed on my left forearm. I was given a shirt and flimsy, striped trousers, jacket and cap. Meals consisted of a brownish liquid for breakfast and watery soup in the evening. Initially I worked unloading coal from rail wagons. We were supervised continuously and urged to work faster. I could see that I would not last long if I stayed there. Using one of the gold coins given to me by my father, I bribed my way into the 'Canada' compound. Its workers had cleaner jobs, better food and warmer clothing. They were housed in a 'showcase' area ready for inspection by the International Red Cross, should the need arise.

Canada compound occupied a building halfway between Auschwitz and the notorious extermination camp of Birkenau. I was amazed by the sheer number of personal belongings that trucks constantly brought in from the Birkenau railway ramps. Our job was to unload the trucks as they came in, open cases and sort contents into separate piles. I needed no ghosts to tell me what had happened to their owners. On arrival, they had gone straight to the gas chambers and crematoria in Birkenau.

At night we worked under bright spotlights. The guards made spot checks when we returned to our camp, looking for smuggled valuables. Trains came from all over Europe packed with Jews who had been 'deported'. When numbers for the gas chambers fell short of their quota, selections were held in the camp. I lived in perpetual fear of being selected or of being taken away for the medical experiments being conducted in nearby laboratories.

I was subsequently transferred to the SS General Stores. Among the items stored, one in particular stands out in my memory. Cans of Zyklon-B crystals were often required for dispatch and were constantly replenished with new shipments.

In January 1945, the Russian army was drawing closer. The Germans began evacuating the inmates. Before their final departure, they dynamited the installations. We were forced to march in a long column, surrounded by heavily armed SS guards. Wearing flimsy clothes, we marched over snow-covered roads in subzero temperatures with no food or water. Anyone who stopped to rest, or even to pick up some snow to drink, was shot on the spot.

The long march came to an end when we arrived in the town of Loslau, where we joined hundreds of other prisoners of many nationalities and were loaded into dirty, open wagons on a coal train. Those who froze to death overnight were thrown out in the morning.

We arrived in Mauthausen concentration camp in Austria on 26 January 1945. I was subsequently transferred to the satellite camp, Ebensee, and then on to Gusen concentration camp where the treatment was even more brutal than before. I suffered tremendously and I had reached the limits of my endurance. I was finally liberated on 5 May 1945, when tanks of the American 11th Armoured Division rolled into Gusen camp.

It took me a long time to recover physically. I was

*Chaim's identity card issued after his liberation from Mauthausen*

emaciated and had a bad infection in my old bullet wound. It took even longer to recover psychologically. I went back to Poland in search of my family, but could find no one. I was just twenty years old and the only member of my family to survive the Holocaust.

Nothing can ever compensate for the terrible loss I suffered or the agony I experienced and it gives me no pleasure to recall these painful memories. But at a time when survivors like me are dwindling in number, it is important to speak out and be heard, for there are people who are trying to rewrite history, to distort the facts or to pretend they never happened.

To talk about Nazi Germany is to revisit a demented period. As terrible as the stories are, they are necessary to remind us of the horrors. We must never forget or we risk having the torch of peace extinguished once more. It flickered and went out during the war.

Never forget. Never again.

§

Following the liberation of Gusen concentration camp by the American army, Chaim found himself too ill to travel, and was taken to a German hospital in Linz to recover. As soon as he was well enough to walk, Chaim began to check the survivor lists that were being posted daily by the displaced persons committee in Linz. Eventually he had to accept that his parents' names would never appear on that list, and that he had no family to return to. While visiting the displaced persons committee, Chaim met Herman Weissalz once more, and was introduced to Isaac, a distant relative.

Before the war, Chaim and his siblings had agreed that if they were separated they would return to Poland

*Chaim (back right) in Straubing with cousins, 1947*

and leave a forwarding address. Dutifully, and without much hope, Chaim returned to Poland. He was still suffering terribly from nightmares and traumatic memories, but the decision to return gave him a goal to move towards.

Zabkowice, the town in which Chaim had grown up, did not offer him a warm welcome. The shops that had been owned by Jews were boarded up. His father's factory was being run by one of the Polish employees, who was suspicious of Chaim's desire to reclaim his inheritance, despite Chaim's assurance that he had no intention of doing so. Even his childhood home was now in the possession of strangers, who had to be talked into letting Chaim retrieve his family's belongings from the attic. The neighbours had no word of his family.

The situation for Jews in Poland after the war was still dangerous. Violence towards Jews who returned was common and many were killed. Chaim witnessed

*Chaim in Straubing, 1949*

the aftermath of a murder when a girl he had known was discovered in the street, stabbed and with a note pinned to her body stating: 'This will happen to any Jew who remains in Poland.' Despite the pogroms, the Polish government made it difficult for Jews to leave the country, and so Chaim and his companions were forced to flee illegally across the border.

On returning to Germany, Chaim, Isaac and Isaac's new wife, Genia, settled in Straubing, where they were allocated a villa that once belonged to a Nazi official. With encouragement from his friends, Chaim participated in setting up a new business – a footwear factory like the one his father had owned.

One of Chaim's suppliers was Helen Wulkan, who showed him a photo of her sister, Rivka. Chaim fell in love with the girl in the photo, and was determined to meet her. Rivka had been incarcerated in various

*Chaim enjoying the beach in Perth*

concentration camps during the war, and was now in rehabilitation in Sweden. Chaim was finally able to meet her when she arrived in Straubing, after being smuggled in by Helen. To his great joy, their feelings were mutual and they married in February 1948. Their son, Sol, was born in November that year.

In the following year, Chaim began to dream of a new start for his young family in Australia. Although they had discussed and had even been accepted for immigration to the USA, Chaim felt that Australia would be safer and provide better opportunities.

Chaim, Rivka and Sol arrived in Fremantle, Western Australia, on 23 November 1950. They quickly made new friends and enjoyed the freedoms offered by life in Perth. However, it was difficult to start a new life in a strange country from scratch. The hot summers were hard to cope with. Work was not easy to find and they had to share a house with their landlady and

Rivka's cousin. Despite these difficulties they were a close and happy family and they made ends meet with resourcefulness and kindness to each other.

Chaim took up many different jobs, working in shoemaking, meat processing and even trying his hand at chicken farming. They saved money and in 1952 purchased a home of their own in Highgate, at last able to fulfil the great Australian dream. In 1955 the Majteles family became naturalised Australian citizens.

In 1957 Chaim opened a new footwear factory, selling his own designs, under the label Regina Footwear. It was a struggle to get the business going, but by the end of the year their finances had begun to improve.

In January 1958 Chaim and Rivka had a daughter, Cyrla Faye. The arrival of this new addition to the family inspired Chaim to buy their first car, an FE Holden, which he drove to the hospital to pick up Rivka, to her surprise and delight!

The following years were prosperous for Chaim's business, and the family built a new home in Mount Lawley. In 1964 Chaim travelled to Israel and met his relatives who had moved there before the war, including his aunts, Leah and Zlata. He was in tears as they embraced him, and felt a tremendous sense of belonging.

From Israel, Chaim returned to Germany, and was amazed by the changes in the country. He was filled with hope that the next generation of Germans were not growing up in an atmosphere of hatred.

In 1980, after twenty-three years with the factory, Chaim decided to retire and sell the business. It was not an easy decision, but was made pertinent by a cardiac arrest that briefly landed him in hospital.

*Chaim and his young family in Perth*

With the support of his close-knit family, Chaim retired and began to take an interest in art. He visited galleries and took classes. Retirement gave him the freedom to read, enjoy music and write his autobiography. He gave talks at the Holocaust Institute of Western Australia, telling the story of his survival to schoolchildren.

Chaim Majteles passed away on 3 April 2004. His son Sol continues to tell the story in his father's place, volunteering regularly at the Holocaust Institute to keep his father's memories and experiences alive.

# Richard Farago

I was born in 1924 in Budapest, Hungary. The city of Budapest is divided in two by the river Danube and the two halves are called Buda and Pest. Pest is largely flat and Buda is the hilly part. The city is connected by a series of bridges. In the Hungarian census of 1941 there were 246,803 Jews just in the city of Budapest. This figure includes 62,350 Jews who had converted to Christianity. This information comes from a comprehensive book about the Holocaust in Hungary by Randolph L. Braham.

My family lived in the Pest area of the city. My father Bertalan Farago was an officer with the railways. Most of the railway clerks in Hungary who had a school matriculation wore uniforms and looked like soldiers. He was one of those – really a Jewish sort of officer.

*Richard's parents on their wedding day*

Those who didn't have a higher education had silver buttons. My father had gold buttons. We were poor, because in spite of all the gold buttons and braid, the job didn't pay a lot. Like many other people, we just lived month to month as the wages came in.

My mother Rudolfine Hirschman was Viennese and had met my father when he was in Vienna on holiday. She did not go out to work. We had a tiny little flat with only two rooms, an entrance hall, a kitchen and a small porch. I lived there with my mother, my father and my older sister Edith, who was born in 1918. We also had the luxury of a servant living with us. Olga Útassy was not Jewish and she helped my mother with the cooking, the washing and the heavier work like bringing up the coal from the cellar. In fact, when we were eventually kicked out from that flat and had to go into the ghetto, she looked after all our things until we came back. She looked after the flat for quite a few years while we were in a different district where all the Jews were herded.

From the age of six until I was ten, I went to a Jewish school. Because my mother was Viennese, the first language I spoke was German. When I began at the school I spoke no Hungarian at all and I can still remember the strangeness of my first days in the classroom. However, I was happy at school, a good student and in a secure environment isolated from anti-Semitism. From the age of ten, I was at a gymnasium, or high school, although not a Jewish one because it was a long distance out in the suburbs and too expensive. Most of our classes were held in the same room and when we were with our form teacher we had to stand and give our name at the beginning of the lesson. When teachers of other subjects such as history, geography or Latin came in we had to stand and give our name and also state our religion. This made me feel self-conscious because I was made to feel different by the sniggering of the other students.

My parents, as far as their Judaism went, were traditional. We had a synagogue called Dohany Templom. We used to go there on Friday nights. We would walk there from where we lived. It was, and still is, magnificent. It was like the Notre Dame Cathedral. They used it as a stable when the Germans were there. All the pews were taken out and they kept horses there but the building stood. It was cleared out and is now back to normal. Next to it is a magnificent and famous Jewish museum. The complex today contains a rabbinical school to train rabbis to work in Europe and elsewhere. There were about 400,000 Jews in Hungary in 1938. The borders changed a lot between 1938 and 1941 as Hungary annexed new territories. Of the 725,000 Jews under Hungary's new borders in

*Richard playing the piano in Budapest before the war*

1941, only about 130,000 were left when the war was finished. Traditionally Hungary was a great centre of Jewish learning.

I loved music and studied piano. I remember playing Liszt, Schubert, Chopin and many others. I was also a boy soprano. There is a photograph I have of me as a young boy at the piano so many years ago in our apartment in Budapest.

After primary school, when I was at the gymnasium, things were still fairly stable. All my mother's relatives lived in Vienna and we visited them twice a year so we were aware of the discrimination against the Jews there. The Anschluss, or annexation of Austria by Hitler, took place in 1938 and my three uncles, who were all engineers with important positions there, were kicked out of their jobs and left the country. The rest of my mother's large family remained in Austria and later on most of them perished in the death camps.

We visited Vienna soon after the Anschluss and

when we returned home my parents decided that I should leave the gymnasium and learn a trade. They felt that this would give me a safer and more secure future. I was fourteen at the time. I went to a technical school and finished there in 1944. It was a five-year course of electrical and mechanical engineering and there were very few Jews in the course.

It was not easy for Jews to study in Hungary. When Admiral Horthy came to power after he had defeated the communists in 1920, the government was very anti-Semitic. They had what they called a *numerus clausus*, which means 'closed number' in Latin. Each faculty at university accepted only three or four Jews. Only the brainiest had a chance to get in. I was not one of them. I knew when I was fourteen that there would be no hope for me to go on. To be a doctor or a lawyer I had no chance. You really had to be a genius – an Einstein – and even then you had to pull strings. You had to know people and it was very hard. Higher education was not for Jews.

When I was at the technical school there was a lot of anti-Semitism. There were only two Jews in our class and regularly there would have been a bashing when you went past a group of students. It became an everyday event. It if wasn't you, then sure enough in a week's time it would be your turn. But you were always able to get yourself a few friends. I had a friend at that school whose father was a communist and when the Nazis came in 1944 he hid me for a while. He was just a worker, a communist in the underground. I was there for a few days.

Open discrimination against the Jews began in 1943 when the Hungarian government, led by Admiral

Horthy, forced the Jews to leave their homes and move into much smaller ones on a share basis with another family. We left our apartment in the care of our family servant Olga, who had been with us all my life, and moved to a different section of the city.

When I finished my engineering studies in January 1944, I was twenty years old. Shortly after that, the Russians advanced south and German tanks and troops invaded Hungary. My age group was called up and we had to join the army. We were sent to a forced labour camp and all the youngsters were given jobs in places where we were regularly bombed by British and American planes. Our job was to repair bombed buildings, roads, sewerage or electricity during the day. By then we always had to wear the yellow armband and yellow star. My mother had the foresight to provide me with a very warm coat and strong boots and these were to stand me in good stead, for we had to sleep in open fields with no shelter of any kind. Eventually I was put in a group of about eighty young men and we were taken back to Budapest where we were housed in a school. Conditions were very primitive and we slept on straw on the classroom floor.

At that stage I had not the faintest idea what was going on in the rest of Europe. When I was still living with my parents, the next-door neighbour had a radio and he turned it up loud and we kids and the whole family would go to the brick wall with glasses to listen to *The Voice of America*. In Hungary it was forbidden to listen to overseas radio programs and the punishment was very severe. Back then occasionally we heard that things weren't going well for the German army and that they were defeated at the Russian front. It wasn't written in any of the papers but it gave us hope. We heard. We knew nothing about what was happening in Poland or Germany. I never heard anything about Auschwitz. We knew that the Jews were taken into the country, herded together and put on trains and shipped away. Where they went, we didn't have the faintest idea.

Life was very difficult but things became much worse when, on 15 October 1944, the real Nazis – called the Fascist Arrow Cross Hungarian Nazis – took over. They had a sign which was two arrows crossed – the Hungarian swastika. Horthy was still there then but they kicked him out. The German SS captured him from his Hungarian castle. They wrapped his son in a carpet and whisked him off to Germany. By that time only the Jews of Budapest were left. Then virtual extermination started in Budapest. It was indiscriminate. Whenever they found a Jew they killed him. The place was full of bodies.

During this time in the forced labour camp I had no contact with my family, but I later learned that my father had been dismissed from work and put in a concentration camp. My father had a brother who had become a Christian and had an important business in the centre of the city. It had been under the patronage of Admiral Horthy. Although my uncle had avoided any contact with his Jewish relatives, when my father was taken away he offered sanctuary to my mother and sister.

Our life in the forced labour camp was very grim and when my sister was able to buy a protective pass from the Vatican, signed by the papal ambassador, and send it to me in the camp, I decided it was time to try to escape. My first attempt at escape in October of 1944 was unsuccessful and I was caught after about an hour

– before I had a chance to reach the sanctuary – and I was taken to a brick factory in Buda.

They were rounding up Jews. There were hundreds of us there. I slept in a kiln. The next day the German soldiers came and they began to take the young men. I said to an officer *'Ich spreche Deutsch'* (I speak German) and I was selected for a work group to work for the German soldiers.

We were taken by truck to another holding area where we stayed for about two or three months. We slept on the floor in a deserted building. There were about twenty of us to a room and it was very cold and extremely uncomfortable. There were no washing or toilet facilities. We were given food, for we needed strength to do the work that was required of us. The Germans plundered Hungary, confiscating mostly food from storage areas, as well as valuables from museums and galleries and from homes and factories, and placing them on barges on the Danube to ship back to German-dominated Austria. Our job was to carry the goods down to the Danube in front of the Hungarian parliament building and load barges with all the stolen goods. Each day we marched about a kilometre to work and loaded all the art treasures, lathes, machinery and various other goods, including mainly food and sacks of flour and sugar, onto the barges.

Many times I witnessed the execution of Jews while I marched to work. One day I was working on unloading a truck full of sacks of food such as flour, sugar and rice when I saw about twenty to twenty-four Jewish people, shackled in groups of three, marching past our truck with guards from the Arrow Cross (or *nyilasok* in Hungarian) to the front, back and side of the group. The first group of three was led down the steps to the

Danube no further than fifty or sixty metres from our truck and made to face the water on the very first step into the river, the water lapping towards them. Then I saw the guard walk behind the person in the middle, pull the gun out of his holster, place it to the back of the person's head and pull the trigger. The middle person was pushed into the water and with that the other two fell in as well as they were shackled together. The guard would wait until the other two came up for air and then shoot them at point blank range. The screams and noise that the other people waiting on the riverbank made was terrible – they saw all of this happening and knew that they were the next ones to be killed in this way.

During that terrible winter of 1944–45 the Danube River was known as 'the Jewish Cemetery'. In 2005 the Hungarian government commissioned a memorial to the Hungarian Jews who were murdered by the Arrow Cross Party on the banks of the Danube. It is called the *Shoes on the Danube Bank* and it consists of sixty pairs of shoes made of iron and scattered on the edge of the water, as if their owners had just stepped out of them. I recently took my family to visit this site, where I had once witnessed these terrible murders and where the monument now stands.

One day, purely by chance, my father was brought into the compound where we were.

We were in the classrooms on the second floor just lying on the straw on the floor and I found him standing in a corner. He was about fifty-four years old then. I barely recognised the man who had been the head of our family. I had looked up to him all my life and now he was a broken person in every sense of the word. I was able to get him to my room and he slept with me.

*Richard at the memorial by the Danube*

He worked with me for the next few days, loading up barges. He could not talk about what had happened to him, but was in a deep depression and cried a lot of the time. It was devastating to witness.

The Russian army was coming closer. We could hear the guns and the bombing. We had a young Jewish group leader and he told us that he had heard that the Russians were about to take over and that the Germans would withdraw their army, taking the Jews with them. At this time, I had still not heard about the death camps and was unaware of what was happening to the Jews of Europe. Nevertheless I sensed great danger and felt that we had to try and escape. I spent all night whispering to my father, trying to persuade him to escape. In the end he agreed and we made our plans.

One morning my father and I loosened our yellow bands. At a certain time when the gendarme was not looking I said, 'Right, this is it,' and ran away from the group. All the other boys saw what I was doing but said nothing. I ran and hid in a pile of rubble. My father was supposed to follow me but he went into the barge and did not come out. I had no chance of going back because I was cut off.

There was a huge square in front of the parliament buildings and my goal was the Swiss consulate, which was close by. Many houses in Budapest had signs out the front indicating that they were under the protection of the Swedish (through Raoul Wallenberg) or the Swiss government or the Vatican. I had papers from the Vatican – the papal nuncio. My mother and sister were still in Budapest. They had false papers and were in hiding. You had to have money or jewellery or friends or people you could trust and you could get a false birth certificate. All you had to do was fill in your name and where it said 'religion' you put down 'Roman Catholic' or another religion. If you were unlucky and you were caught by the police and asked for your papers, you had to show them and sometimes you got away with it. If you were a man, they forced you to drop your trousers, as Christians were not circumcised. Luckily, I was never cornered. I was in the forced labour camp and there was no need for it.

I escaped from the Danube working party and went into the Swiss consulate.

To this day I have always wondered how I got there. It was a terrifying day for me. Soldiers were patrolling the streets and I knew I would be shot on sight. It took many hours to reach the consulate, although it was only a short distance – one that would normally have taken only about twenty minutes to walk. Because I had removed my yellow star and yellow armband, they could have taken me as an army escapee. There were many people trying to get in; I was lucky and succeeded. I carried with me my Vatican pass and at the gate of the consulate I showed it to the guard to prove that I was a genuine Jewish escapee.

There was a hidden staircase and a trapdoor leading to the stairs. Inside there were three thousand Jews in hiding. The Swiss consulate was called 'the Glass House' and at least one book has been written about it. This was also where the Judenrat (leaders of the Jewish community who were forced to liaise with the Nazis) had finished up. The Nazis knew that Jews were hiding there but the Judenrat had paid them an enormous sum to leave them alone. Eventually, the negotiations between the Judenrat and the Nazis broke down and as the Russians approached the centre of the city, the Jewish leaders were taken out and executed by the Germans.

I was at the Swiss consulate for two months – hidden in the cellar the whole time. The Jews were lying in tiers like you see in the films. Eventually I got a job cleaning the latrines and for that we received an extra ration. It was like damper – bread made with just flour and water. Everybody got one piece of damper and a bowl of soup which was just cold water with bits and pieces of vegetables floating in it. If you cleaned the latrines you got an extra piece of damper. That was all for the day. It was enough. It sustained you. You didn't die. You lost a lot of weight but you lived.

I stayed in the Glass House until January 1945, when the Russians liberated us. When the Russian soldiers came down to the cellar with their guns they couldn't believe their eyes. There were three thousand Jews like ants who came out from the cellar. It was miraculous.

We poured out of the consulate into the street and were free.

I knew where my mother and sister were hiding and I started to walk there through the snow. By this time my boots were worn out and my feet were bound in rags. I was emaciated and weighed only forty-eight kilograms. On the walk, which was not long, I passed a burnt out bakery without windows. There I saw huge piles of Jewish bodies, with their yellow stars still attached. Apparently two days before the Russians liberated Pest, the Germans had received instructions to murder all the Jews. As I walked along the snow-filled streets, I came across a group of bodies lying in the snow. They had been shot and I was shocked to recognise one of them as an old family friend.

Eventually I reached my mother and sister. They were hiding in the cellar of a building in the inner city which belonged to our uncle. He was also taken away and we never saw him again.

Although Pest was liberated, the Germans in Buda were holed up in the castle in the hills, which had been the headquarters of Admiral Horthy, and they held out there for another month. During this time the Russians were indiscriminately arresting any able-bodied men they found in the streets. They didn't care if one was a Jew or not; they had to have numbers. Every day they had to capture 'enemy' soldiers. They just picked people up and they were forced onto trucks. Thousands of Jews finished up in Russia and never came back. Every day the army communicated the number of 'enemy soldiers' they captured. Some of these could have been Jews picked up from anywhere – wherever they found them. So it was very uncertain. The war was still raging.

My mother and sister were so resourceful. A bomb had struck the building next to the Swiss consulate when we were down in the cellar and I had a small wound on my forehead. My mother and sister bandaged my whole head completely, as if I had a very large wound, to protect me from the Russian soldiers. One day I was stopped by three or four Russian soldiers. They asked me what was wrong with me and I said, 'A German bomb.' Luckily they didn't take my bandage off.

We had no money and how we survived, only God knows. In the Swiss consulate there was food – there was soup and flour because the Hungarian leaders had a deal with the SS. When the war was finally over we went into the countryside and traded. We hitched rides from Russian soldiers and bartered whatever we had – clothing and whatever we could find. We went to farms and the peasants gave us bread or fat, which we brought back to Budapest. Once the war was over, we returned to our original home and found that our family servant Olga was still there. She was overjoyed to see us and we were equally happy to see her. She was part of our family and I had known her all my life.

I heard about my father's fate later from a friend who had survived. After my escape, as the Germans evacuated Pest for Buda, my father and the whole group of forced labourers were taken from the barge to the railway station where my father had worked for the last twenty-five years. They were bundled into cattle wagons and eventually stopped at the Hungarian border with Austria, which is at a village called Hegyeshalom. There the doors of the cattle wagons were opened and the group had to march towards Mauthausen concentration camp, which is just past Linz in Austria. My father got as far as Bruck an der Leitha, which is approximately fifty kilometres inside Austria. As he was walking across the frozen snow-covered fields his legs gave up. He could not walk any more and he collapsed. One of the guards got off his horse, went to my father and with his rifle butt, smashed his head in. This was told to me by two of my friends, Bardos Zoli and Weisz Gyuri, who were there in the group with my father. They survived Mauthausen and, on returning home, said to me, 'You will not see your father again.'

I went to Austria with my wife many years ago to talk with the mayor of the city to see if I could exhume my father's body, bring him back to Perth and give him a decent, proper Jewish burial. We found out that there was no way to do that, because he is buried in a mass grave. Instead the mayor gave us a document in which it is stated exactly the date of my father's death and the 'cause' of it.

My father had a very large family living in the country. They were all rounded up and sent to Auschwitz. Not one survived.

Life in Hungary was not easy after the war. In July 1945, I was able to get a job in an electrical factory called Tungsram. I still had no shoes and walked with my feet bound with rags. It was a long way to walk to work and sometimes I was able to hitch a ride in a horse-drawn cart that was loaded with produce. It was forbidden for soldiers to give lifts to us Hungarians and if the driver saw an officer approach in a car I was quickly turfed out or hidden under sacking on the cart.

My sister got a job in a government department and through her I received a permit to obtain shoes and other items of clothing. I still have the authorisation – dated 26 October 1945.

In February 1946 I became very ill at work and I was placed in a sanatorium to recover. I remained there for over six weeks until 12 April, and then continued working in the factory. Around this time, conscription also began and my age group was called up to the army by the Russians. All the people who were born in 1924 had to report.

My mother and sister and I decided that we must leave Hungary. My mother's brother Max Hirschman had left Vienna after the Anschluss and migrated to Australia. After the war he had been in touch with the

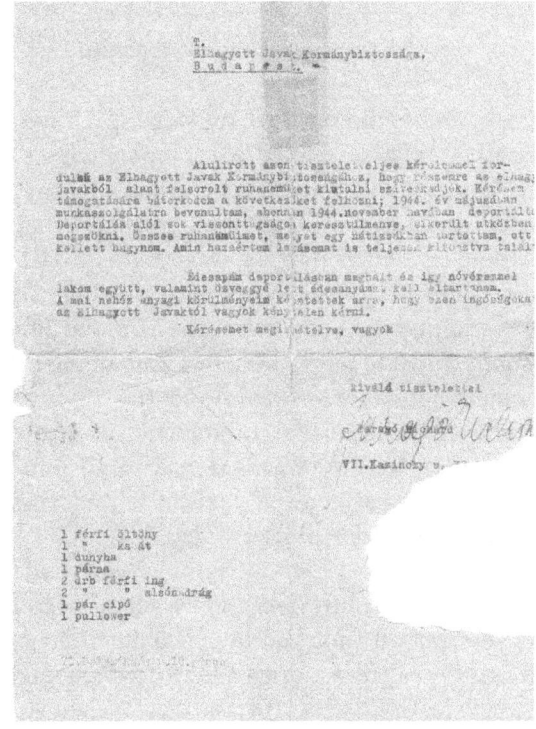

*Authorisation to receive clothing after the war*

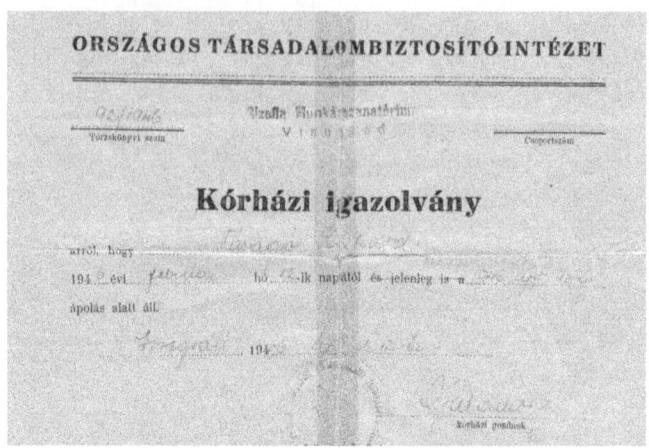

*Hospital admission document from 1946*

Red Cross and found out that we were still alive so he and another relative named Mr Zinner helped us to arrange the paperwork we needed to come to Australia. I needed to have a job waiting for me and prove that none of us would be a burden to the Australian government. That was an edict of the prime minister Ben Chifley. Mr Zinner found me a position at the Midland Junction workshops. I had to work there in a kind of indentured government job for two years and the Immigration Department checked on me throughout this whole time and for two years afterwards. I had to go into their office on Murray Street and register my address in a little booklet which I still have today.

We left Budapest in July 1947 and we got as far as Paris. Our travel was all financed by the Joint Distribution Committee. Wealthy American Jews donated money to help people leave Europe after the war. We got stuck in Paris because the ship wasn't ready and we had to wait

*Australian immigration booklet*

there for three months. There were masses of refugees in Paris. The Joint Distribution Committee paid for the hotel and the food and they even gave us clothes. They allowed us to enter a huge warehouse where I picked out a jacket, trousers and shoes. Finally we left for Australia. It was a long journey – around six weeks.

We arrived in Australia on 4 November 1947 and were met at the Fremantle docks by the Zinners and their young daughter Hannah. Of course I couldn't speak a word of English. We stayed with the Hirschmans in their home on the corner of Regent Street and Clifton Crescent. There was the family Hirschman, the family Zinner and the family Schreiber. It was a big house but it was so full – there was a little dog as well. I remember on the first day I arrived, they gave me a drink. I had never had Coca Cola in my life and I thought it was magnificent. They told me not to drink too much or I would lose my teeth! That was the first day in Australia and I was very impressed.

*The Midland Railway building*

Later we stayed with a couple called the Lederers on Galway Street in West Leederville. They allowed us to stay and sleep on their verandah for about three months. There were three beds on the verandah that they had set up for us. After that we moved to 117 Forrest Street in North Perth. Again we were on the verandah – people always allowed us to stay there.

January came and I was allowed to start work at Midland. I would go to the city and then by train to Midland Junction. When I started working, I couldn't understand a word that people were saying. The foreman would tell me to sweep the floor and I would just stand there. He had to put a broom in my hand and show me what to do and slowly I learnt English that way. Those people were very decent. I think I was the only foreign worker there. It was a huge workshop – there were three thousand people working there. Our workshop dismantled steam engines. They would teach me the names of the tools by drawing pictures of them –

*Richard and Auriel on their engagement*

hammer, chisel, nail – so I got to learn English.

When I arrived in Perth I was introduced to a lot of German-speaking people and when they found out that I had been a boy soprano in Budapest they asked me to come and sing in the choir at the old Brisbane Street shule. A stalwart of the Perth Jewish community, Mr Masel, would pick me up in his car from the corner of Forrest and Fitzgerald streets in North Perth and take me to the shule. In those early days, I also sang in the choir for the West Australian Opera Society. I performed in *La Traviata* and in *The Tales of Hoffmann*. Hanz Briner was the conductor and we had all of our rehearsals at his home on Rokeby Road in Subiaco.

I met my wife Auriel when I was invited for lunch at the home of the Cohen family. Auriel was living in Melbourne at that time. She had come home to visit and her family had invited this young Hungarian migrant boy around. I played the piano and Auriel was very

*Richard and Auriel on their wedding day*

impressed. I was around twenty-four or twenty-five then. Auriel went back to Melbourne and we started corresponding. My English was terrible and she must have laughed her head off but she wrote back.

My contract with the Midland workshops expired and I needed to find other work. I still couldn't speak English well. I went to the university and showed them my electrical engineering diploma from Hungary and asked if I could take it again. They looked at the papers and told me that I couldn't. I was too old to become an apprentice and would have had to start from scratch, so I couldn't follow my trade, nor could I go back to study. I had to earn money. There was no one to fall back on.

Around that time, I'll never forget one of the elders of the Jewish community coming to me and telling me not to stay in Perth but to go to Melbourne because there were more opportunities there. So I moved to

Melbourne, taking my mother with me. My sister was already living there.

I found a job with a section of the Main Roads department. I had to paint traffic lights. They gave me a ladder and a brush and I had to scrape the lights back and paint them. The work was outdoors and it was fine in the summer and spring but when the winter came I got a terrible cold and became very ill.

Then I worked for an insurance company called Employers' Liability as an interpreter. It didn't matter who came in – I had to translate. I can only speak three languages but luckily most of the Europeans spoke a little German. I then started working for the Shell Oil Company in Newport. I had to count drums ready to be shipped off on trucks. Every day at three o'clock I had to ring Head Office to report on the figures. I also sang in the choir at the Toorak shule. They paid me well to sing – one pound a week.

I married Auriel Cohen at the Toorak shule in March 1950. Our daughter Michelle was born in 1952 in Windsor. Auriel always wanted to return to Perth because the weather in Melbourne was so awful and also her family was in Perth. Shell was good enough to transfer me to the Shell depot in Fremantle. Our second daughter Vicky was born in Perth in 1953 and our third daughter Wendy was born in 1957.

Soon after Auriel and I returned to Perth we joined the Temple David congregation. We were members up until 1975 when the Perth Hebrew Congregation shule was built in Mount Lawley and we switched over. In all that time at Temple David I sang in the choir.

One day, as I rode on the bus to work in Fremantle and it stopped on the corner of Bay View Terrace, I noticed

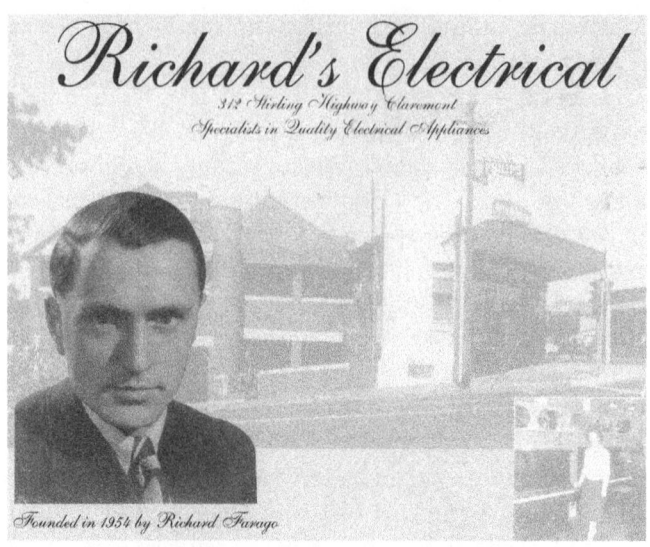

*Early advertising for Richard's Electrical*

the electrical goods store there. I saw on the corner a sign saying it was for sale. I went back home to talk to Auriel. I am an electrical engineer and I wanted to buy that shop but I didn't even have two cents in my pocket.

I went into the National Bank in Claremont and spoke to the manager. A friend, Bertha Finkelstein, told me to approach the bank manager – it was sheer chutzpadik! The bank manager asked me what I had as collateral. Did I own anything? Nothing. He told me to find someone to guarantee the loan for me and he would give me a thousand pounds to buy the shop and a small overdraft. I asked Auriel if she thought her father would guarantee me and she said, 'No way!' I had never even been in business before. But she nagged him for a couple of weeks and he agreed. I didn't go broke for sixty years, so he was grateful for that. And that's how I started my business – really with no money at all.

I opened my business on the first of July 1954. In those days my name 'Farago' could not be pronounced by Australians so I decided to call the business simply Richard's Electrical. When we first opened, there was barely anything in the shop – absolutely no stock at all. There were only four or five second-hand radios and two or three fridges. I was a fleabite and there was huge opposition – lots of national and local companies competing with me. But I was able to manage somehow, mostly through the customer service I offered. I would go and pick up people's toasters and irons and have them repaired and then redeliver them. A friend of mine had an electrical repair workshop and they would do the repairs for me. I think that sort of service got me going. In the beginning only one person would come in a day. I was penniless.

Then I applied for and received three months credit. I ordered a lot of light fittings. I had about fifty light fittings and I lit them all up and suddenly people started coming. In the third month I was able to pay back some of the credit but things were still very slow. In the second or third year I employed a woman to help at the shop. When it was hot we shut the shop and took our bathers and went down for a swim at Peppermint Grove, then came back by 2 pm. We didn't miss out on any business because it was so quiet.

Then in the late 1950s television first became available and people everywhere were desperate to get hold of black-and-white televisions. They even traded in their pianos to get them. Soon my shop was full of pianos. I had a French polisher who would restore them and we would sell them. The piano I have today is from that time.

Soon I had at least half a dozen salesmen working for me. No wife wanted to sign the papers until her husband was home so the salesmen would visit people at their homes each evening from 5 pm to 11 pm. Each of them would make five or six sales and twenty or thirty sets had to be delivered the next day. We sold a huge number of televisions. It was an enormous operation. I opened other stores in Wellington Street in Perth and in Rokeby Road in Subiaco, as well as a showroom in London Court.

I also had the Claremont store, which I began to expand. Bit by bit, I bought out all the other stores on the block and broke through the walls to expand my shop. I demolished one building to create a big parking lot because I realised I would never have business unless I had enough parking for customers. Then we realised we didn't have enough storage space so I employed Max Hardy the builder and he dug out an area beneath the building and supported it with steel girders to make a huge storeroom. Eventually, the great TV panic calmed down and I closed the stores in Subiaco and Perth.

I had to work very long hours. I left for work at seven in the morning and came home at six or seven at night. Even on the weekends I brought home paperwork – my bedroom was my office. The shop closed at 12 pm on Saturdays, so on Saturday afternoons and Sundays we would go on picnics. Our girls attended Coolbinia Primary School and Mount Lawley Senior High School. On Sundays they would go to Hebrew school.

Eventually we bought the house we were renting in Holmfirth Street in Mount Lawley. We had a traditional home. We were members of Temple David and we

*Richard and his daughters in the 1970s*

celebrated all the Jewish festivals. Sometimes I would conduct communal Seders for other families in the neighbourhood too.

In the 1960s Retravision approached me to ask if I would be interested in joining them. Retravision had formed in 1959 in Australia to allow small businesses to formalise their purchasing power into a buying group. At the time I didn't know if it was a good or bad thing to do but I went ahead. Retravision became a huge national organisation with about five hundred stores across Australia. We had enormous buying power and the store did very well for many years. Auriel would come down and help in the office and for a time my daughter Vicky was a salesgirl too. I was on the board of Retravision for sixteen years and attended many meetings in Perth and Sydney.

I wanted to contribute to the Australian community

*Richard with his family in Perth in 2014*

and have been involved in a range of volunteer organisations for many years. I joined the Rotary club of Claremont-Cottesloe in 1967 through Dr Jack Bercov, Rex March and Arthur Hatfield and was a committed Rotarian member for thirty odd years. I was president of the Rotary club of Claremont-Cottesloe from 1981 to 1982 and I received a Paul Harris Award in 1991. In the early 1990s I was approached by Ken Crew, then Rotary president, telling me I was nominated for District Governor of our District 9450, but unfortunately I had to decline this great honour, because just at that time I had a mild heart attack and my doctors advised me not to take up the appointment.

In the early 1960s I became a member and fundraiser for the Jewish National Fund (JNF). I was involved with the JNF until 2000 – nearly forty years – and from 1995 to 1999 I held the position of president. During my presidency, I was approached by the Israeli consul general at the time, Mordechai Yedid, and the Egyptian consul general, Nabil Ibrahim, to create a Peace Grove in Western Australia in memory of Israeli prime minister Yitzhak Rabin and Egyptian president Anwar El Sadat, who were both assassinated for their courageous efforts to bring about peace. Establishing the memorial was not an easy task. I approached various councils with no success but eventually I received support from the then lord mayor of Perth, Dr Peter Nattrass, and the Peace Grove was created. It was officially dedicated in Arden Street, on the banks of the Swan River in East Perth, on 8 February 1998. Large numbers of people attended the opening ceremony – not just from the Jewish community but from the Egyptian community as well.

Soon after the Holocaust Institute of Western Australia opened, I became involved as a volunteer and shared my story with many school students in Years 11 and 12 from all over Perth and from the country as well. Some of the teachers who accompany the school groups tell me that they had heard me speak when they themselves were students. Still today I give talks to many school students.

Recently I have been involved in the organisation of the Courage to Care initiative, which is an educational program that seeks to recognise those brave people who risked their lives to save Jews during the Holocaust, and to empower the younger generation to stand up to discrimination and injustice.

In 1972 I made my first trip back to Hungary. I felt terrible. When I went to the house where we lived in the ghetto it was a terrible feeling. Auriel never liked it. She felt very uncomfortable. I could not ring my friends. All those people I spoke to years ago were scared to talk – some of them were Communists. The city was beautiful but it was not a pleasant journey. It was a sentimental journey and I wanted to go back and see what my old country looked like.

When I went back in 1977, it was slightly better. In 1980 it was a lot better.

When I go back now I really only go to the opera because Budapest has a beautiful opera house. All my relatives have gone. They are all gone – all perished, all killed off during the war.

My wife Auriel has passed away now but I have my three daughters and seven grandchildren.

## Hanoch (Heiny) Ellert

I was born in 1922 in a small town called Neustadt in Lithuania. There was a relatively large Jewish population. Neustadt had been part of Germany before the First World War and so there was still a big German presence there. We all spoke German and we lived among Germans and they treated us relatively well. It was only later, after Hitler's rise to power, that we felt things really begin to change for us.

I was the middle child of three. My sister Lena, born in 1921, was only eighteen months older than me. There is only one photograph that survives from my childhood and it shows Lena and me dressed in our winter coats and hats. My younger brother Hirschel was born in 1927. I do not have a photograph of him.

My father was a butcher and when I was about three

*Heiny's mother Pesia, aunt Henna and father Michael, c. 1920*

years old we moved to a larger town called Heydekrug where he opened his own butchery and also a factory for making polony. I can remember being allowed to put the kosher stamp on the meat, which made me feel very important. We lived close to the German border and my father sold a lot of kosher polony to Germany.

My family was a traditional religious one and I remember a happy, comfortable childhood. There were only about thirty Jewish families in Heydekrug and only ten Jewish children, but at that time we were still considered part of the community. I went to a German primary school and I don't remember any discrimination as a small child.

Of course when Hitler came to power in 1933, the year I turned eleven, life for us began to change. All sorts of anti-Semitic measures were introduced. Young people went around singing the song of the Nazi party and I remember my parents' anxiety. Still our lives went

*Heiny (right) with his sister Lena before the war*

on and we endured it as best we could. We could not have imagined what was ahead of us.

By this time I was in high school, which was taught in Lithuanian. We spoke German at home, like everyone else in the region, and I had to learn to study in a new language. In 1935 I turned thirteen and had my bar mitzvah. It was not too long afterwards that things began to get worse for us.

In 1938 Germany had already started annexing parts of Europe. The borders changed and Germany took back control of the Memelgebiet, which was the district that included Heydekrug. All of the Jewish families left and moved further into Lithuania. My family returned to Neustadt where my father was able to open a butchery.

When I was seventeen I left for Kovno to study at a Jewish trade college called ORT. I wanted to become an electrician. The motto of ORT is 'Educating for Life'.

I did not realise it at the time, but what I learned there would ultimately save my life. My skills as an electrician were valuable during the war. They made me useful to the Germans and in the end they were what made the difference between being sent to the gas chambers or being allowed to live. Studies at ORT were conducted in Yiddish, which I had to learn. That was another skill that would come in handy later on.

The war broke out during my time at ORT but I continued to study initially. When war was first declared in September 1939, Hitler had a pact with Stalin and the eastern part of the country where we lived came under Russian control. It was only when Hitler decided to turn on Russia in 1941 that the true nightmare began for us.

On 22 June 1941 the German occupying forces marched into Neustadt at five in the morning. I was home with my family for the summer holidays. My father was arrested and sent to work in a forced labour squad in Heydekrug. During the German invasion there were some skirmishes with the Russians and several soldiers were killed. Along with some other young Jewish men, I was made to bury four German soldiers who had been killed in the fighting. When I was returning home I saw German soldiers forcing people to burn siddurim and sifrei Torah (Jewish prayer books) in the schoolyard. None of us could believe what was happening, that people we had lived among could turn on us like this. The German commandant barking orders at everyone was Mr Shade, a local baker my family had been buying bread from for over fifteen years.

Two weeks later we were forced to leave our homes and we were herded into a ghetto, along with all the other Jewish families of Neustadt. The ghetto was overcrowded and chaotic and there was no privacy. My mother, my younger brother Hirschel and I shared one small room. We had no clothes or blankets and my mother begged Mr Shade to allow us to return home to collect the things we needed. My sister Lena had been visiting relatives in another town and was forced into a ghetto there.

Conditions in the ghetto were terrible and the Jews living there had no rights. We were not allowed to walk on the pavement, only in the street or in the gutter. A dog could walk on the pavement, but not a Jew. The Germans tried to strip us of all our dignity, to make us feel that we were less than animals.

On 19 July 1941 a directive was issued by the Germans for all Jewish males over the age of twelve to assemble in the yard of the shule. Once again my mother asked Mr Shade for mercy and he agreed to allow my brother Hirschel, who was fourteen, to remain in the ghetto with her. All the other men who had been rounded up were marched to the stables of the old Russian garrison.

An SS soldier demanded that all tradesmen step forward. There were twenty-seven of us with useful skills and we were told that we were going to work in Germany. I was eighteen years old and my life of forced labour had begun in earnest.

It was the middle of summer and we were all wearing shorts and sandals so we were given permission to collect some other clothes. Back in the ghetto I said goodbye to my mother and Hirschel. I had no idea what would happen to any of us but I wanted to stay hopeful for their sake. I told them that perhaps I would meet up with my father, who we had not seen since he had been taken away a month earlier, and that we would work together. That same day, as I was on my way back to report to the SS, a friend told me that he had seen my father travelling by on a tractor from Heydekrug. I missed seeing my father by five minutes and I have regretted all my life that I had no chance to say goodbye to him. I never saw my father or my mother or my brother again.

I heard later that my father had been taken to the Jewish cemetery and shot by the German killing squads, helped by some Lithuanians. Apart from our small group of skilled tradesmen, all the Jews of Neustadt met the same fate. My mother and my little brother, along with all the other women and children and the unskilled and elderly men, were taken to a forest near the town and shot. They were buried in mass graves. The officer who ordered this murder was SS Reich Sturmbannführer Dr Shoy.

The next few years were a time of relentless, brutal forced labour, deprivation and hunger. I started off digging stormwater channels through the farms in the Heydekrug district, living in barracks with the other men from my town. Conditions were very difficult and although we were doing heavy physical work, we were given very little food. Fortunately for me, I had never been a big eater, and I think that is what allowed me to survive for so long on so little. It was so much worse for those with strong appetites. One day a Christian German woman gave me a sandwich. It contravened all the Jewish dietary laws but it was delicious.

There was rollcall twice a day where all the prisoners were counted. A Jewish man named Monas Kagan, who had been a lieutenant in the Lithuanian army, was given the task of counting us and reporting to the guard in military style. The first German guard was young and did not treat us too badly. However, he was soon sent to fight at the front and we were allocated a wounded SS soldier who was very cruel.

Each day our beds and clothes were inspected military style and if everything was not perfect we were whipped or caned. One day my bed was not up to army standard so we were all assembled in the dining room and whipped. As the SS guard beat me with a leather cane, he struck something in the pocket of my jacket. He found my ORT textbook, which had my picture in it. Inside the book I had two articles from a newspaper on the German front. This made the guard furious. He got very red in the face and threw me onto a bench and started striking me repeatedly, yelling, 'You are a spy!' After some time he stopped, but for weeks I was unable to sit down or sleep on my bottom.

The winter came and we were moved to Heydekrug, working in different places. Some of us worked in the brickyards belonging to the SS Reich Sturmbannführer Dr Shoy, who has been the officer who ordered the mass murder of the Jews of Neustadt, including my parents and brother. In the brickyards, our guard would often get drunk and issue orders to entertain himself. Among our group was a father and his two sons. One day the guard ordered them to crawl on their stomachs through water and mud. The father and one son obeyed him out of fear but the younger son tried to avoid the water. The SS guard became angry and pulled out his revolver and shot him in front of us.

That incident remains indelibly in my memory but it was just one of many awful things the prisoners had to witness. We were always hungry and one day a young man called Reuven hid outside the camp and went to a nearby house to beg for bread. He was caught and brought back and the next day we all had to assemble in the yard and watch while he was hanged.

The winter was cold and wet and we were desperately hungry all the time. We never had enough food. A horse died on Dr Shoy's estate and was buried. A group of prisoners asked permission to dig it up again to cook and eat the meat. We never had meat and I remember that we were so grateful to be able to eat the flesh of this dead horse. It was the first time we had eaten meat since being taken prisoner.

Around this time a new dairy was being built in Heydekrug and electricians were needed. The German contractor was an old man who had known my family before the war. He told me that he had begged my father not to go home on the day of the German round-up in the summer of 1941, but that my father wanted to return to the family so he did not listen to the warning and begged Dr Shoy to let him go home.

Another Jewish prisoner called Itzke Mureinik and I worked together on the dairy, installing all the lights and motors and wiring the mechanical cheese churns. We worked a lot in the ceiling of the dairy, putting in cables. One day we stole a ten-kilogram round of cheese, cut it in half and hid it in our toolboxes. Every day we took it into the ceiling and ate a piece. The old German man knew that we had stolen it but he said nothing. We were very lucky as people were killed for less. There was a Belgian prisoner of war working with us. He was a welder and he sometimes received Red Cross parcels. One day he was caught with a litre of cream that he had taken from the dairy. The following day he was hanged.

When we had completed our work at the dairy we were sent to work for various farmers in the region. This went on for around two years until July 1943 when we were marched to the railway station and herded into cattle trucks. Each car was so crowded that there was standing room only, and we were all packed tightly together. The journey took ten days, in the middle of a sweltering summer. There was no food the whole time. Once we were given water but everyone was so thirsty that they fought to get some water and most of it was spilled on the floor. I did not receive a drop. People were so desperate that they began to drink their own urine. I will never forget one moment of that terrible journey.

Our destination was the Auschwitz-Birkenau concentration and extermination camp. Of course we did not know then what it was. The doors of the cattle wagons opened and there was a selection process. Some people were ordered into a big, closed van with a red cross on it, others were spared and then marched into the camp. I remember seeing the sign *'Arbeit macht frei'* ('Work makes you free') above the entrance and thinking perhaps that things would be better for us. Then we saw the smoke from the chimneys and smelt the burning flesh.

We were given numbers, no names, and they were tattooed on our arms. The number 132703 was tattooed on the outside of my forearm but Dr Joseph Mengele declared that it was not visible enough on my sunburned skin so he ordered a second tattoo.

It was summer and incredibly hot in Birkenau. Whenever it rained people tried desperately to drink water from the ground. Doing this, they caught malaria and were ordered into the gas chambers and then the ovens. My best friend Itzke, who I had worked with for so long, caught malaria. He came to say goodbye to me before he was sent to the gas chambers.

There were more and more selections and more people were chosen to be gassed. A friend of mine called Phil, who was a tailor, had wounds on his feet like me. We would put green leaves on our wounds to protect them from the dirt. Before the selections I would take them off and I begged Phil to do the same. He told me that he did not care and that we would never get out of there anyway. During that selection we had to line up in rows and the SS man walked among us. He took one look at Phil and said, 'You with the green leaves – come out.'

There was also regular *entlausing*, or lice-checking. At night we would be ordered to stand outside in the cold in rows. We had to take off our clothes, which were only striped pyjamas labelled with our camp number, and throw them into a hole in the ground. A

*Heiny's bunk in Block 16a at Birkenau*

*Heiny's tattoo*

floodlight was shone on the hole and our clothes were hosed down with fluorine to kill the lice. Then the people in charge checked the numbers and returned our clothes. Sometimes it took hours to get our soaked clothes back. We put them on and went to sleep in them. When we woke in the morning the clothes were still wet.

By this time we were skeletons. We were fed only half a litre of watery soup each day and a slice of bread in the evenings. There was barely any drinking water or water to wash with. Conditions were terrible and when the summer ended it turned cold and dark. Some people committed suicide by throwing themselves against the electric fence. I don't know where I got my will to live despite everything. Part of it was because I wanted revenge. I wanted revenge on Dr Shoy, the officer who had ordered the mass murder of all the Jews of Neustadt. After the war people helped me to see that this was futile, that

I should give up my desire for revenge. It would not help anything.

In October 1943 we were marched out of Birkenau. We were all so weak by this time and those who could not walk fell down on the road during the march. They were shot and left by the roadside. We arrived in Warsaw and were housed in more barracks. This was after the Warsaw Ghetto Uprising and our job was to clean out the destroyed ghetto. I worked in an electrical commando unit. We had to dig out and dismantle electrical transformers, which were then sent to Germany.

A typhus epidemic broke out in our camp and I became very ill. I woke up in a kind of hospital. I don't remember how long I was there but when I came out everyone was surprised to see me. They all thought that I had died a long time ago.

I was put back to work and, in June 1944, I was sent to Dachau. I was only there for a few days but there was no food. While I was there I met Issy Lichtenstein, who I knew from Lithuania.

Soon I was moved to Mühldorf where I was sent to work on a building site carrying cement and iron bars. I was at the end of my strength by this time but I carried on. There were no SS men and no soldiers there and things were a bit better for us. We worked cleaning the camp and the work was not as exhausting as before. Sometimes we heard planes flying overhead. There were blackouts then and we knew that the war must soon be over as it must be bombing by Germany's enemies.

One day a new group of men from Shavel arrived in the camp. I was amazed to see that my cousin Herman

Ellert was among them. Herman introduced me to a man names Jecheskel Galperin, who he told me was my brother-in-law. He had married my sister Lena. I was dumbstruck because I had not heard from my sister in years. I had no idea that she was even still alive. Jecheskel told me that on leaving the Shavel ghetto, Lena had been separated from him and sent to another camp. The men from Shavel only stayed with us for five days before they were sent on to another work camp called the Waldlager.

One day not long after that we were marched out of the camp and put in cattle trucks again. The train took us from Mühldorf to Munich. When we arrived the doors were opened by German guards who told us that the war was over, and then disappeared. Everyone was bewildered. We didn't know what to do or where to go. We could not believe that we were finally free.

Soon afterwards the Americans arrived and we were sent to a displaced persons camp run by the United Nations Relief and Rehabilitation Administration (UNRRA) called Feldafing. For the first time in four years I had enough to eat. At Feldafing I worked guarding the storeroom, which was filled with clothes and shoes.

After all I had been through I didn't want to be Jewish anymore. I wanted to give up my faith. I wanted nothing to do with it. I didn't want to go to a shule, or even walk past one. But outside the camp there was a large Magen David. I don't know why it was there but something changed when I saw it and I decided that I must go back to being Jewish. That it was the wrong thing to do to turn away from that.

I had been in Feldafing for about two months when

*Heiny (right) in front of the Star of David
at Feldafing displaced persons camp*

some soldiers from the Jewish Brigade (a Palestinian Jewish unit of the British army) came through the camp asking people if they wanted to go to Israel. I had no one left, I didn't know if anyone had survived, so I took my few belongings and jumped on their truck. We were taken though Austria and across the Alps to Italy, where we stayed for a while in another UNRRA camp in Santa Maria di Bagni on the coast. We relaxed while we stayed in holiday villas there. There was no furniture and we slept on the floor but we were happy because we were free and we had enough to eat. We also enjoyed swimming in the sea. Sometimes we swam two kilometres to a nearby town to see films.

One day some new people arrived at Santa Maria di Bagni and told me that my sister Lena had arrived in the Feldafing camp. I could not believe that she

*Heiny with friends after the war*

*Heiny (right) with friends after the war*

was still alive. She was the only remaining member of my immediate family and I had not seen her for more than four years. I wanted to go back to Germany to see her and, with two others who also wanted to return, I hopped on a train to the Austrian border. The trains

*Heiny (right) and a friend after the war*

at that time were always full so we just held onto the sides of the carriage. We had to hike through the Alps. It was winter by then and I remember sliding on my bottom through the snow. Eventually we were found by an Austrian ski patrol. We had been told to say that we had come from Germany so that they would send us back there rather than returning us to Italy.

It was wonderful to see my sister Lena. I had thought that she had died like everyone else. Some of my other extended family had also survived – Herman, Moshe, David, Eda, Israel, Judith and Masha. They had all been in Shavel when the war broke out.

I worked in Germany for several years, first at the UNRRA food magazine and then at an electrical firm in Munich called Siemens-Shukert. While in Munich I worked in Hitler's theatre, which had been

*Heiny after the war*

bombed during the war. I worked for a German firm and nobody spoke about the war. They knew I was Jewish but they never said anything. When I finished working for them they gave me a letter of reference. I worked hard and was able to support Lena and her husband Jecheskel, buying extra food coupons so that we could all eat well. We all lived together in Feldafing, Lena and Jecheskel in one room, me in another. Lena and Jecheskel's first child Michael was born there.

Later I was given the position of Camp Engineer at Feldafing. It was during this time that I first owned a car – a Volkswagen that had belonged to one of the senior German foremen. I was the only Jewish man with a motor car and they certainly were a bit jealous of me.

I didn't want to stay in Germany though. In 1949 Lena and her family decided to move to Israel and so I went with them, sailing to Haifa from Venice. Through some cousins there I found work with the electrical contractor Asher Feuchtwanger. I was a foreman with ten electricians working under me. I also served in the army for one month every year. At that time we didn't have enough tanks so we used mules. We would load them up with ammunition. When we were on patrol the mules got fed first and then we got to eat.

It was in Israel that I met my wife Toby Mann, who had come to Israel from South Africa on an ulpan program to study Hebrew. She was also from Lithuania originally but her family had left in 1937 for South Africa. It was lucky that I had learned Yiddish because Toby didn't speak much Hebrew and I didn't speak English, so we spoke Yiddish. We met in August and by Rosh Hashanah in September Toby called her parents to tell them that

*Heiny and Toby's wedding day in South Africa, 1954*

*Heiny's store in South Africa*

*Toby and Heiny with their sons*

we were engaged. They helped me to emigrate to South Africa.

We lived in Johannesburg for two years, where our first son Harold Hirschel was born in 1955. Soon after we moved to Witbank where we opened our own business. It started as a general dealer store and then became an electrical business called Ellert's Electrical and TV. Our second son Larry was born in 1959 and our daughter Shana in 1964.

After some time, all our children moved away from

South Africa. In 1986 our daughter Shana, her husband Duddi and children Meidan and Dana moved to Israel. That same year Harry and his wife Deborah and their two children Dana and Alyssa moved to Perth. Larry and his wife Anne and their children Sarah, Ariella, Michi and Jonathan followed and relocated to Perth in 2000.

We had almost no family left in South Africa. Toby's parents and sisters had died and my uncles and cousins had also gone. Two of our sons and six of our grandchildren were in Perth so we followed them there in 2006 and we have lived here since. This year we celebrate our sixtieth wedding anniversary. Our family is very important to us.

I don't ever want to go back to Europe. The only reason I would want to return to Neustadt is to say Kaddish at the mass graves of my family, but I will never do that now. I can't forget anything that happened. Still, today, I do not understand it. It will never leave me.

The Holocaust is still happening every day, all over the world, in places like Syria and Lebanon. There are still wars, mass killings and discrimination between mankind. People don't treat each other the way they should and it's for this reason the Holocaust is still going on.

The Holocaust is a monumental part of history, so please do not forget what I am saying. I won't be here forever to tell the story. It is in your hands and the hands of your generation and generations to come – to always remember.

*Extensive research was conducted by Michael Ellert and Rebecca Brest as part of their Year Ten Living Historian Project at Carmel School, Perth, in 2012. Zoe Brest also contributed significantly to this project.*

*Heiny with his family at his eightieth birthday in 2002*

*Heiny with his grandchildren*

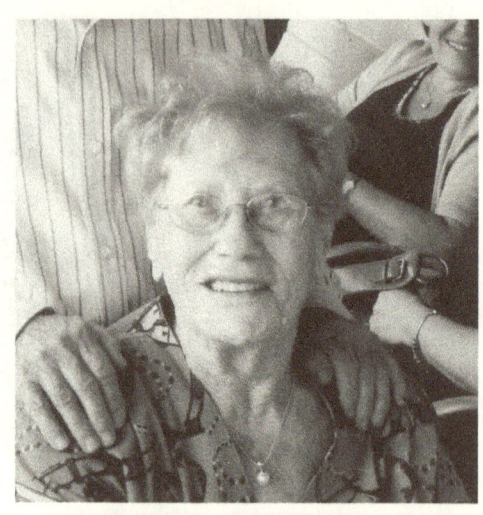

## Pola Potaznik

I was born in Radom, Poland, in 1923. Radom is a town about one hundred kilometres from Warsaw and its population included many *Volksdeutsche* – people of German origin who had settled in Poland but retained their German identity. I was one of five children – one boy and four girls. My brother was the oldest – three years older than me. I was the second oldest. We were a very happy family. My father worked at home preparing leather cut-outs for shoes.

When I was a young child, times were very hard because of the Depression. There was widespread poverty in Poland but things did begin to improve towards the end of the 1930s. After completing primary school, I stayed home to help my mother and to learn dressmaking.

Then the war started. In September 1939, the Germans invaded Poland. I was sixteen at the time. It didn't take long until the war reached us. During an air raid, a building in the next street was bombed and my father went to help dig out the dead bodies. Soon after he returned, a German soldier knocked on our door and took him away at gunpoint. With the help of unsympathetic Poles and *Volksdeutsche*, all the Jewish men in our building were being identified and rounded up. When I saw what was happening I hid my older brother under a blanket. My father told us afterwards that he and the others were taken four kilometres away to check an area for landmines. A German officer arrived and asked what was going on. The soldier in charge replied that the Jews were being used to clear the area of mines and were to be killed afterwards. Through what can only be described as a miracle, the officer instructed the soldier to release the men. My father walked home. This was the day the Germans arrived in Radom.

Life immediately became more difficult. To obtain food, we had to stand in queues for long periods of time. Usually all that was available was one loaf of bread per person. The Germans would often pick Jews out of the queue with the help of Polish children and force them to go without. I didn't look Jewish so I usually managed to stay in the queue. Later the population of Radom were issued with ration cards for food. The Jews had different cards from the others and received much smaller rations.

Soon after arriving, the Germans began seizing Jewish men at random to work as slave labourers. The men would disappear in the morning and return at night exhausted. They were forced to perform hard labour and were often beaten. On one occasion, my father was so badly beaten that it took him a week to recover.

In 1940, the Jewish community was forced to form a Judenrat, or Council, which was answerable to the Germans. The Judenrat was forced to provide a daily supply of Jewish slave labourers. Sometimes my younger sister and I would go to work in place of our father and brother. We were taken to the German officers' quarters and forced to clean their homes.

Trains often passed through Radom packed with Jews from Western Europe. My father spoke with some of the passengers in Yiddish and found out that they were being taken to the east 'for resettlement'.

In 1941, we were informed by written decree that two ghettoes were to be set up in Radom. All Jews were ordered into one of the two ghettoes and were forbidden to venture out. We were forced to wear a blue Star of David prominently displayed on our left sleeves to identify us as Jews. A high wall was built around the Jewish section of Radom, near the synagogue. Outside it was guarded by Polish police. The wall enclosed an area that included our home. Three other families moved in with us and we lived one family per room. Food was scarce. On presentation of our ration cards we would receive a small loaf of corn bread daily. It was meant for four people. We also had some food stored from beforehand but others were not so fortunate. Children would steal out of the ghetto and risk their lives trying to smuggle in potatoes and other vegetables that could be obtained outside. Occasionally our diet would be supplemented with soup made from smuggled food. People became swollen from hunger. Many died in the street.

A friend of mine worked in an army store. It was called AFL and was about one kilometre away from the ghetto. My friend arranged for me to work there repairing army uniforms. Every morning I was allowed out of the ghetto and walked to work.

On 5 September 1942, Polish police and German soldiers came into the ghetto during the night and began driving people out of their homes. There was a teeming mass of people assembled outside. I was with my mother and youngest sister. My mother told me to save myself – that I was safe because I had a place to work. I did not want to leave her but she insisted. I started running but I didn't know where to go. I heard voices and police shot at me repeatedly. The assembled Jews were being separated into two groups. I finally stumbled into one of the groups. People in the other group were herded into cattle trucks. We heard from Ukrainians and Poles who went with the transport as guards and drivers that the Jews had been deported to Treblinka. I never saw any of them again.

When I came home, I found my father and my brother there. My mother and two of my sisters were gone. My father was crying. It was the first time I had ever seen him cry. He told me to return to AFL as I would be safer there. The next day, the AFL workers were taken to have a shower near the assembly point for the deportations. I was horrified to see that the ground was moving. People had been shot during the round-up and buried while still alive.

I lived in a barrack at my workplace. I never saw my father and brother again. They were taken away in the second deportation, along with my remaining sister.

Early in 1943, the Judenrat posted notices urging people to register for emigration to Palestine. A lot of people registered and were taken away in black cars. We learned afterwards from some Jews who escaped and returned to the ghetto that they had been taken to a nearby village called Szydlowiec. Ditches had already been dug there. Except for a handful who escaped, they were all killed.

In April or May of 1943, we were sent from AFL to a concentration camp at Blizyn. We were transported there in sealed cattle trucks. The trip took about four hours. The camp was surrounded by a barbed wire fence. There were German guards in raised outposts at regular intervals around the perimeter. It was impossible to escape.

I was put to work repairing uniforms. There were all sorts of jobs, primarily aimed at supporting the German war effort. These included mending uniforms and military boots, working in stores and repairing roads. There was very little food. We would be given a slice of bread and jam for breakfast and then work from 8 am until 5 pm. At midday, we had to queue to receive a plate of watery soup. In the evenings we were given a second slice of bread.

At night I slept in a huge block which housed thousands of women. We slept on planks which were stacked five high. We continued to wear the clothes that we had with us on arrival. There was no distinct uniform. Inmates were beaten or shot for trivial things.

There was a rollcall every evening. One night I was sick and came a few minutes late. As punishment, I was ordered to stand outside in the subzero temperatures all night. It was a miracle that I survived. On 8 November 1943, all the children in the camp were rounded up and taken away. I was twenty at the time.

Typhus was widespread in the camp and I contracted

it and became very ill. I was admitted to the camp hospital where Jewish doctors looked after me. There was a meagre supply of medicine. The sick were fed extra soup made from leftover apple peels thrown away by the Germans. I stayed in Blizyn for fourteen months.

In August 1944, I was transferred to Auschwitz-Birkenau locked in a sealed cattle wagon. The journey took two days. It was dark and there was no food, no toilet facilities and barely enough room to stand shoulder to shoulder with others on the transport.

We arrived at nightfall. I could see a huge camp surrounded by electrified barbed wire fences. We were met by other prisoners and taken to be showered. Our hair was shorn and we were given uniforms. Mine was a flimsy dress with no stripes. The letters 'K.L.', standing for *Konzentrazion Lager*, were stamped on the back. We were then taken to a barrack for women. The next day the number A15335 was tattooed on my left arm.

We were housed in the women's barracks in the Birkenau death camp. I did not work. Some of the prisoners in my barrack, particularly doctors and nurses, did have work but it was usually of a minor nature. We were fed a plate of watery soup, a piece or two of bread and a cup of coffee daily. There was no soap to wash with and no warm clothing. Winter was approaching and we were cold and hungry.

Transports would arrive regularly, day and night, in a never-ending stream. Sometimes from a distance I would see the new arrivals marched away. They would never be seen again. Mostly when the transports arrived, we were forced to stay inside our barracks. Sometimes we were allowed to walk around outside. I could see huge chimneys in another part of the camp. It was always possible to smell burning flesh. We learnt from Jews working there that the chimneys belonged to the crematoria. People from the transports were burned there after being killed in the gas chambers nearby. We were told that the corpses were inspected and gold teeth removed before cremation. Their hair was saved and the body fat was collected to make soap.

On one occasion, I saw a transport of sick and frail people arrive from Lodz, a city in the west of Poland. About twenty of the new arrivals were marched half a kilometre to a freshly dug trench. A liquid, presumably gasoline, was poured over them and they were set alight.

I spent each day numb with fear, thinking only about how to survive. Prisoners were regularly picked out at rollcall for laboratory experiments. After the war I met a friend whose mother had been selected in this and was sterilised. I was lucky to survive three of Dr Mengele's selections. Other inmates were selected for execution. We would see them being led away by a group of musicians playing mournful tunes on their instruments.

Towards the end of my stay at Auschwitz-Birkenau, I spent three weeks in the Auschwitz concentration camp. While there I was forced to push a wagon filled with rubbish. I was very weak and found it almost impossible. I was beaten so severely by a woman guard that my left eardrum was perforated, needing numerous operations after the war. It was unwise to report sick in the camp. People simply disappeared from the hospital, never to be seen again.

I stayed in the death camp for about six months. In December 1944 I was included in a transport of three hundred women prisoners who were sent to work in an ammunition factory near Leipzig in Germany. We worked very hard assembling firearms. There was very little food. On Sundays, when we didn't work, we were given a plate of soup made from *brukiew*, a vegetable used in Poland to feed cattle. On other days we were given two slices of bread – one in the morning and one at night.

In the spring of 1945, the Americans were approaching. We were evacuated by rail. German soldiers occupied the passenger carriages in the front of the train and we were crowded in cattle wagons behind. We stayed in these wagons for four weeks. All we had to eat was half a cup of beet sugar each day. Those who collapsed were given a little water. There were no toilet facilities. People relieved themselves where they stood. We couldn't wash and the stench was unbearable. Many people lost their self-control and lashed out at the smallest provocation. A few girls died during the journey.

With the Americans closing in, the German guards arranged for the train to be taken over by the Red Cross and then fled. We were taken to a ghetto in Theresienstadt. The ghetto was now being run by Jews, the German guards having fled. I was swollen from hunger and so sick that I couldn't even walk. Although more food now became available, I developed large festering sores under my arms. I was in agony. I was then sent to a sanatorium for two months and my health slowly improved.

In May 1945 the Red Army arrived and we were finally freed. The Polish government encouraged us to come back to Poland so I returned, hoping to find some trace of my family, but there was none.

The Polish people were openly hostile towards the

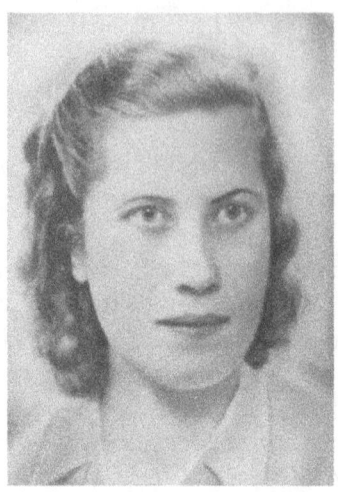

*Portrait of Pola after the war*

Jews returning from the concentration camps and emerging from hiding. There were three pogroms around this time – attacks by the local Poles against Jews. Many Jews were killed.

§

Pola remained in Poland for several years after the war. However, life became increasingly difficult. Her home town, so empty of Jews, was full of tormenting memories and it was almost impossible to continue living among the Polish people who had mostly cooperated so enthusiastically with the Nazis and who still lashed out at the survivors returning from the camps.

After the war Pola had met and married another survivor and decided to attempt to escape Poland to migrate to Israel, which had officially been established as the Jewish homeland the year before, and where they hoped to have a better future and build a family. They did not have permission to leave Poland and when they were crossing the border, guards spotted them and shot Pola's husband, killing him. Pola was jailed and discovered that she was pregnant with her dead husband's child. After her release, her son Nathan was born.

Despite the fresh disaster that had befallen her, Pola carried on with her son and made the journey to Israel, settling in Tel Aviv. She had escaped the open anti-Semitism and traumatic daily reminders of Poland, but life in Israel as a single mother with no family or friends and a young baby to care for was very difficult. Conditions in the fledgling nation were challenging, with strict rations and housing shortages as the flood of refugees from Europe descended upon the country. Pola tried to find work to support herself and her child, as well as attempting to learn Hebrew.

In 1956, Sam Potaznik, who had known Pola's family in Radom before the war and had migrated to Western Australia, heard about Pola's difficult situation in Israel and offered to help her come to Perth. Sam had survived the war by escaping from Poland into Russia and had lived in a displaced persons camp in East Africa for seven years before travelling to Australia. A tailor by trade, Sam's skills at making safari suits had been in such demand in the displaced persons camps that the commandant had been reluctant to give him permission to leave.

Sam sponsored Pola to migrate to Australia and they were married shortly after her arrival. Sam raised Pola's son Nathan as his own child, and in 1957 the couple had a daughter, Anne. Boarding with another family

*Pola and Sam Potaznik in Australia*

in Maylands, Pola and Sam worked hard to establish a tailoring business, saving money until they were able to buy their own home in Yokine. Pola attended English classes and devoted herself to becoming a talented homemaker. She was a dedicated and loving grandmother to her five grandchildren and in her later years she and Sam moved into a granny flat on her daughter Anne's property.

Pola never returned to Poland. She could never reconcile herself with the fact that so many Polish people had participated in the murder of the Jews. She continued to observe her faith, keeping a kosher home and attending shule. After all she had lost, the Jewish observance of Yizkor became very important to her. *Yizkor* means 'remember' in Hebrew and is recited in the synagogue four times a year on Jewish holy days.

Pola rarely spoke of her experiences during the war. There was not a day when the horror of what she had been through did not press on her, as well as her guilt over being the only one in her family to survive, but she wanted to shield her children from the terrors of her past. She also felt that Australians did not want to hear the awful details of the Holocaust. It was too foreign and too awful a subject to speak of.

When she was invited to share her story with students and visitors at the Holocaust Institute of Western Australia, she agreed because she saw it as another way to honour her family's memory, to reanimate and remember all those she had lost.

Despite her reluctance to return to the country of her childhood, which was filled only with horror for her now, Pola was immensely proud when her youngest granddaughter Michal travelled to Poland as part of the March of the Living to visit the sites of the death camps, to honour those members of her own family and all the Jews who had been murdered there. Michal later became a youth leader for the March of the Living, guiding groups of young people through the intensely confronting experience. For Pola, it was a symbol of the endurance of memory. Her family had died anonymously, with no one to observe the formal rituals of mourning for them, but they would not be forgotten.

Pola passed away aged eighty-six in 2008.

# Glossary

| | |
|---|---|
| aliyah | Immigration of diaspora Jews to Israel (Hebrew word literally meaning 'ascent' or 'going up'). |
| bar mitzvah | The ceremony celebrating a Jewish boy's thirteenth birthday, which marks his acquisition of religious obligations (Hebrew phrase literally meaning 'son of the commandment', referring to the boy himself). The equivalent ceremony for Jewish girls is called bat mitzvah ('daughter of the commandment'), celebrated at age twelve. |
| chutzpadik | A Yiddish term meaning shameless audacity or extreme self-confidence, but generally used in a positive sense. |
| gefilte fish | A traditional Jewish dish made by poaching minced fish. |
| Hanukkah | A Jewish festival that commemorates the liberation and rededication of the Temple in Jerusalem by the Maccabees after its desecration by the Seleucids. It is marked by the kindling of eight candles and known as the Festival of Lights. |
| Hebrew | A Semitic language, used in its classical form for Jewish prayers and ceremonies. |
| Joodse Raad | The Jewish Council established by the Nazis in the Netherlands in 1941 and made responsible for implementing German orders in the Dutch Jewish community. |
| Judenrat | Jewish councils or administrative bodies established on the orders of the Nazis in occupied countries during World War II. The councils were forced to carry out German orders and regulations and had no authority of their own. |

| | |
|---|---|
| Kaddish | A Jewish prayer recited by mourners after the death of a close relative. |
| kibbutz | A communal Israeli settlement, traditionally agricultural, which is owned by its members and founded on principles of collective ownership of property, social justice and equality. |
| Kiddush | A traditional blessing recited over wine on the eve of the Jewish Sabbath or a Jewish festival. |
| kosher | Food that satisfies the requirements of Jewish dietary law. |
| kreplach | A traditional Jewish dish consisting of small filled dumplings, usually boiled and served with soup. |
| Magen David | A six-pointed star that has come to be a symbol of Judaism. Also known as the Star of David. During the Holocaust, Jewish people were forced by Nazi decrees to wear a Star of David badge. |
| matza | Thin unleavened bread traditionally eaten during the Jewish festival of Passover. |
| menorah | A seven-branched candelabrum that was located in the Temple in Jerusalem, and became a symbol of Judaism. The nine-branched candelabrum used during the Jewish festival of Hanukkah is known as a 'Hanukkah menorah'. |
| mitzvah | A Jewish religious obligation (Hebrew word literally meaning 'commandment'). In common usage, however, it often refers to any good or meritorious deed. |
| Passover | A Jewish festival commemorating the exodus of the Israelites from slavery in Egypt. |
| Pesach | The Hebrew term for the Passover festival. |

| | |
|---|---|
| rabbi | A Jewish religious leader. |
| Righteous Among the Nations | An official term used to refer to non-Jewish people who helped to save Jewish lives during the Holocaust. Those designated as Righteous Among the Nations are formally honoured by Yad Vashem, the Holocaust memorial in Jerusalem. |
| Rosh Hashanah | The Jewish New Year festival. |
| Seder | A Jewish ritual service and ceremonial dinner held on the first night (or, if celebrated outside Israel, on the first two nights) of the Passover festival. |
| sefer Torah (plural: sifrei Torah) | A sacred scroll containing a copy of the Torah (holiest Jewish text), kept in a synagogue and used during religious services. |
| Shabbat | The Jewish Sabbath, observed from sundown on Friday to sundown on Saturday. Traditionally families gather for Shabbat dinner on Friday evening. |
| shiva | The traditional Jewish seven-day period of formal mourning observed by close relatives of the deceased. |
| Shoah | A biblical Hebrew word that translates as 'catastrophe' or 'disaster' and is used to refer to the genocide of the Jews of Europe under the Nazi regime. |
| shochet | A person officially certified to kill animals for meat in the manner prescribed by Jewish law. |
| shule | The Yiddish word for a synagogue. |
| siddur (plural: siddurim) | A Jewish prayer book containing prayers according to the order of the Jewish calendar. |
| sukkah | A temporary shelter with a roof of branches built during the Jewish festival of Sukkoth |

|  |  |
|---|---|
|  | and used especially for meals during the festival. |
| Sukkoth | A Jewish festival that commemorates the sheltering of the Israelites in the wilderness during their exodus from Egypt. |
| ulpan | A school for the intensive study of Hebrew. |
| underground | Another name for the various resistance movements that worked against the Germans in occupied European countries during World War II. |
| Yad Vashem | The world centre for documentation, research, education and commemoration of the Holocaust, based in Jerusalem, Israel. |
| yarmulke | A skullcap worn by Jewish men. Orthodox Jewish men wear a yarmulke at all times while the non-Orthodox wear it only during prayers. |
| Yiddish | A Germanic language written with Hebrew letters, spoken mainly by Jews in central and eastern Europe and their descendants. |
| Yizkor | A memorial service and prayer for the dead recited in the synagogue four times a year on Jewish holy days (Hebrew word literally meaning 'remember'). |

# Acknowledgements

This book belongs to the fourteen survivors whose narratives are included here. These are their stories and their memories. Without their enormous bravery in sharing their experiences and their dedication to the production of this collection, this book would not exist. My sincere thanks to all those who agreed to contribute their stories.

Grateful thanks also to the many family members of the survivors who assisted with the preparation of these narratives, providing vital information, helping to fill in gaps and generously sharing their memories and reflections, as well as giving permission to include the photographs, images and documents reproduced in this collection. I would like to recognise the generous assistance of Maud Debreczeni, Norma Ehrenfeld, Toby Ellert, Ben Glatzer, June Grynberg, Kerry Grynberg, Max Grynberg, Peter Grynberg, Anne Levitt, Sol Majteles, Eva Migdalek, Martin Moen, Charles Niesten, Jessica Niesten, John Urban, Michelle Urban OAM, Wilma Piller and Frank Rothschild.

Thank you to Dr Ben Korman OAM and the staff and volunteers of the Holocaust Institute of Western Australia who, over the past two decades, have invested immeasurable time and energy in documenting and recording the experiences of Holocaust survivors in Western Australia and in facilitating the sharing of these stories with the wider public.

I am indebted to Jenny Shub OAM and Skye McAlpine Walker who worked alongside me throughout the process of producing this collection. Their passion, dedication and sensitivity have been invaluable. Jenny worked with many of the survivors when the Holocaust Institute of Western Australia was founded to assist them with the painful process of recording their stories in the form of written testimonies. Skye's skills as a research assistant in updating and extending the narratives have been essential to this project.

Thank you to Jane Fraser and the staff of Fremantle Press for their belief in the importance of preserving these stories and their masterful shepherding of the publication process. In particular I would like to thank Naama Amram for her skilled and sensitive editing of the collection, her scrupulous fact-checking skills and general wisdom. Thank you also to Deb Fitzpatrick for her brilliant proofreading skills.

Many thanks to Arnold Zable for his careful reading and beautiful foreword.

### Further acknowledgements

Important additional information was obtained from Kurt Ehrenfeld's interview with Melanie Schwartz for the Survivors of the Shoah Visual History Foundation.

For Heiny Ellert's narrative, extensive research was conducted by Michael Ellert and Rebecca Brest as part of their Year Ten Living Historian Project at Carmel School, Perth, in 2012. Zoe Brest also contributed significantly to this project.

A version of Erica Moen's narrative was originally published in the historical collection *Without Regret*, edited by Louise Hoffman and Shush Masel, Centre for Migration and Development Studies, the University of Western Australia, 1994. An early, briefer version of Richard Farago's narrative was also included in this collection.

Rosalie Rothschild's narrative has been adapted from a longer, self-published account of her wartime experiences and has been included here with the kind permission of her family.

I am grateful to Leah Kaminsky for giving permission to quote from her beautiful poem 'My daughter goes on camp' from her collection *Stitching Things Together*, published by Interactive Press in 2010.

The quote from David Grossman in the introductory essay is from his 2003 book *Death as a Way of Life: Dispatches from Jerusalem* and is used with the kind permission of Bloomsbury Publishing, London.

The Elie Wiesel quote is from his essay 'Art and the Holocaust: Trivializing Memory', published in the *New York Times* on 11 June 1989. It is used with the kind permission of Georges Borchardt Literary Agency.

www.ingramcontent.com/pod-product-compliance
Lightning Source LLC
Chambersburg PA
CBHW021145160426
43194CB00007B/691